GOOD
THINKING

GOOD
THINKING

TEACHING ARGUMENT, PERSUASION, AND REASONING

ERIK PALMER

STENHOUSE PUBLISHERS
PORTLAND, MAINE

Stenhouse Publishers
www.stenhouse.com

Library of Congress Cataloging-in-Publication Data
Names: Palmer, Erik, 1953-
Title: Good thinking : teaching argument, persuasion, and reason / Erik
    Palmer.
Description: Portland, Maine : Stenhouse Publishers, 2016. | Includes
    bibliographical references.
Identifiers: LCCN 2015044683 (print) | LCCN 2015045259 (ebook) | ISBN
    9781625310644 (pbk. : alk. paper) | ISBN 9781625310651 (ebook)
Subjects: LCSH: Thought and thinking--Study and teaching. | Reasoning--Study
    and teaching. | Persuasion (Rhetoric)--Study and teaching.
Classification: LCC LB1590.3 .P325 2016 (print) | LCC LB1590.3 (ebook) | DDC
    370.15/2--dc23
LC record available at http://lccn.loc.gov/2015044683

Book design by Blue Design, Portland, Maine (www.bluedes.com)

Manufactured in the United States of America

PRINTED ON 30% PCW
RECYCLED PAPER

22 21 20 19 18 17 16   9 8 7 6 5 4 3 2 1

To my debate coaches at Greendale High School and Southern Methodist University for their contributions to my lifelong obsession with good thinking

CONTENTS

ACKNOWLEDGMENTS

When I started this book, I went to the Twitterverse to find out how teachers were teaching argument and reasoning. It seems that many brilliant teachers have Twitter accounts and use those to connect with others who share a commitment to becoming better, more effective educators. Quite a few were willing to assist me. They covered a wide range of grade levels and subject expertise. They included teachers from around the globe—from Cathy, five miles away, to Teresa, a teacher at an international school in Hanoi. I was amazed at their enthusiasm and desire to help. Several of these teachers shared activities you will discover as you read the book; others contributed ideas to help me verify that I was on the right track. I thank all of them: Jessica Lifshitz, Colleen Kires, Erika DeShay, Cathy Walker-Gilman, Mark Bowden, Bill McBride, Lindsay Metcalfe, Paul Solarz, Kaitlyn Fischer, Sandy King, Donald Kreienkamp, Laura Wagenman, Megan Kelly, Andrew Smith, Paul Bogush, Dave Stuart Jr., and Teresa Winterstein. This book is better because of you.

I also found Sandy Otto on Twitter. Sandy has a few educators and authors that she calls "edu-heroes"—people who have inspired her and positively influenced her teaching. Sandy is *my* edu-hero. She is passionate about education and constantly striving to be better, though it is clear, after visiting her classroom, that she is already a master teacher. I bounced ideas off her to get a practitioner's view of things. She tested lessons so I could see my ideas in action. She offered wonderful suggestions and encouragement. And she had a wonderful openness to new ideas. Education needs more Sandy Ottos. Her contributions to this book are invaluable.

For a third time, I find myself thanking Holly Holland, my editor extraordinaire. She made *Well Spoken* better, she made *Digitally Speaking* better, and she made this book much better. Holly helped me brainstorm the ideas and structure of the book before a word was written, and polished up the manuscript after all the words were written. She is a great editor and friend.

My wife, Anne, is mentioned in the book a few times. She is a fantastic teacher and artist. Her lessons show up in the text, and she drew Figure 3.3 for this book. Of course I thank her for those contributions. I also thank her for holding dinner because I had to get some ideas down, checking in during long writing sessions to see if I needed anything, and listening as my "target market" and giving feedback. Without her support, this book might never have happened. Anne is the best person you could have on your side.

CHAPTER 1

Introducing Good Thinking

"Not everything is an argument!"

Those were the exasperated words of my father. You see, I joined the debate team in high school. The debate team profoundly changed my life . . . for the better. Debate involves researching, collaborating with partners, thinking critically, and performing under stress. Of course, debate also demands strong speaking skills, and as readers of my other books know, I am passionate about developing oral communication skills in all students. But the part that changed my father's life for the *worse* was that debate is also about reasoning well. I never quit practicing.

Yes, Dad, I could take out the garbage, but let's look at that more closely. First of all, perhaps you are unaware of the women's lib movement, but there is no reason why certain jobs should always fall to males. Why not ask one of my sisters to do this? Additionally, you lead a sedentary life in an office. Research indicates that exercise is good for health, and though it is only mild, taking out the garbage does provide some exercise and would be good for you. I care about you and want what is best for your health.

Perhaps you can understand his exasperation.

He was no doubt correct: not everything is an argument. However, many definitions of the word *argument* contain phrases such as "suggesting reasons to persuade others." If we use that meaning, it is certainly true that a large part of our communication *is* argument. We often try to convince people that an idea should be adopted. For example, we try to convince

- a spouse that it's a good night for pizza instead of leftovers.
- the principal that more passing time is needed for students moving through hallways between classes.
- the staff that the new initiative is good for everyone.
- our students that they should work hard on the assignment.
- our children that they should clean their rooms.
- the store personnel that they should honor the coupon even though it is one day past expiration.

Many times a day, we try to reason with others. I'll wager that at least once a day you think, *What? That's crazy! They are way off!* when you see or hear something that you think is unreasonable. Not a day goes by without us calling on our reasoning skills. We analyze the messages we receive. We reason with others. We even reason with ourselves: *Should I eat that doughnut? Explain, conscience.*

THINKING IN SCHOOL

How well do students think?

We usually answer that by pointing to some kind of score: Kim got all the answers right on the quiz; Roberta correctly edited her paper. They must have done some good thinking. What really went on, though? Kim did a nice job of *remembering* facts or procedures; Roberta did well *remembering* and *applying* the rules of our language. We test recall and application of facts and procedures all the time, but those are only two aspects of thinking.

How well do students apply analytical or argumentative or logical thinking? How effectively do they analyze information presented in diverse media? Can they critically analyze a speaker's point and point of view? How well do they construct an argument? These tasks all require *reasoning* rather than remembering. When we look carefully at our students, we notice that their reasoning skills are not what they need to be.

When I taught eighth-grade civics, I didn't want my students to memorize random facts: the Articles of Confederation were adopted

November 15, 1777; a bill is handed to the clerk and placed in the hopper; the executive branch contains departments, independent agencies, and government corporations. I wanted them to see government as a living thing with real connections to their lives. I found that many topics in the curriculum led to lively discussions:

- What is the purpose of government?
- Should the government provide health care?
- What are the responsibilities of citizens?
- Should citizens have to pass a test to qualify for voting?
- What are the rights of citizens?
- Should students have those rights also? If so, should a school be able to punish a student for something done outside of class?

The discussions certainly inspired thought and, often, strong emotions. They also revealed many reasoning errors. For example, we once discussed a case involving a student who was suspended from school for making posts on a social media site. The posts were made outside of the school day but referred to other students at the school. The conversation follows:

DAVE: No one should get in trouble for something done off school grounds.

DERRICK: I know, right? What is this, Nazi Germany?

LATRICE: But lots of suicides happen from when someone said a bad thing about someone else on Facebook, you know. Shouldn't schools stop suicides?

SONJA: I don't care if someone says something bad about me. Facebook comments aren't a big deal.

Reflecting, we can see that every comment demonstrates an error in reasoning (and I note the chapter in this book where that type of error is discussed):

- Dave: a conclusion with no reasons provided (Chapter 4)
- Derrick: loaded words (Chapter 6)
- Latrice: no evidence for claim (Chapter 5) and derailing the train of thought (Chapter 7)
- Sonja: generalizing and derailing (Chapter 7)

These errors were not entirely their fault. I taught students about the Bill of Rights, but when did I teach them how to think and reason well? Of course, I could excuse them by noting that impromptu speaking is difficult. No one had time to prepare a well-thought-out statement. But what about students' writing? How did they do when given more time to think?

I asked students to write a Twenty-Eighth Amendment to the United States Constitution and explain why it should be adopted. Our Constitution has been amended twenty-seven times since its adoption, and I suggested that perhaps other changes are needed. I challenged students to think of a change they would like to see. One student thought that California should have more senators than North Dakota and wanted to change Senate membership. One thought the right to bear arms in the Second Amendment should be eliminated. Another wanted to eliminate the Electoral College. In spite of all the time they had to research and develop their reasons, the students showed specious reasoning skills. For example, an essay about the Electoral College contained these statements:

> First, the Electoral College was created a long time ago. Things have changed since then. Eighty-four percent of all polling places have electronic voting now so the Electoral College is not needed. *(evidence does not match reason, Chapter 5)* Second, Al Gore was the better candidate and should have won the presidency. *(prejudice, Chapter 7)* Why didn't he? Because of the Electoral College. Finally, small states don't get much of a say in the election. We only get nine votes but California gets fifty-five. Is California six times as good as Colorado? No. *(misusing facts and figures, Chapter 7)*

It was clear to me that I needed to spend some time working on students' reasoning skills. I wondered whether other teachers were thinking the same thing.

Fortunately, I know some other teachers, one of whom lives with me. My wife, Anne, teaches fourth grade. I knew that students in middle and high schools were asked to create arguments and demonstrate good reasoning, but at what level do we ask this of younger students? I was curious about what could be expected in elementary school, so I asked Anne for some help. She was quick to point out that, on a daily basis, her students were doing the same kind of thinking I was asking of my students. She shared an example from her classroom about *Time for Kids*. She uses that magazine in her class and told me about the debate column that's in every issue. One issue's debate topic asked students to discuss whether commercials for fast-food restaurants might lead to childhood obesity. Her students had these responses:

My mom says that fast food is bad for you. (testimonial, Chapter 6)

Have you seen that one commercial where the guys fight over that one sandwich? (derailing, Chapter 7)

I eat lots of fast food and I'm not fat! (generalizing, Chapter 7)

I watch TV and I don't eat fast food.

You do too! We went to McDonald's after soccer last week! (derailing, Chapter 7)

Just 'cause you watch TV doesn't make you fat. It depends how much you eat.

From these examples, I could clearly see that young students (a) love to engage with issues, (b) are asked to do high-level thinking, and (c) are capable of reasoning but need guidance just as older students do.

So where are the materials for teaching these skills? You have a scope and sequence for math, a science curriculum, a language arts program, and more. Is your school like my wife's, with no materials for systematically and specifically teaching good thinking and reasoning? In preparing to write this book, I used social media to ask educators to contribute ideas about how to teach good thinking. It turned out to be a nonscientific study verifying that most of us feel unprepared for the job. These comments were typical:

> *My district has not done any professional development on argumentative writing.*
> *The school system has little instructional resources on argumentative writing.*
> *I have no real experience with argumentative writing.*
> *I have limited instruction in teaching argumentative writing . . . My school has not provided me with any materials to help with argumentative writing.*

How, then, can we be expected to teach thinking?

THINKING OUTSIDE OF SCHOOL

I decided to create my own resource file. What real-life models are available?

Because I had a career in the commodity trading business before I went into education, I am still in the habit of checking financial news. When I took a break from writing, I turned on the TV and saw a commentator on the floor of the New York Stock Exchange.

> *I have never liked the president [bias], and everything he does proves me right [confirmation bias].*

I flipped to a sports channel. (I know. I should stop procrastinating and get back to work.) A commentator was complaining about the National Basketball Association's collective bargaining agreement.

> *How can you expect anything other than a comment like that from him? This guy is one of the dumbest guys in sports! [attacking the person]*

The next channel had an ad. What are ads? Attempts to use reasons to change your behavior. A car commercial had gorgeous people and beautiful images surrounding the car (transference) and nothing about the features of the vehicle (lack of evidence).

Disappointed with the reasoning I had witnessed, I decided to look to see how an online discussion was going. I posted a response to a blog that was very critical of state standards. The original blog was on a site for educators. An excerpt from the discussion:

> **ERIK:** With which standards do you have a problem? Be specific. For example, is there a math standard at some grade level that you think is wrong? A speaking standard that is off base?
>
> **BLOGGER:** Why are you defending the standards? [changing the burden of proof]
>
> **ERIK:** I didn't defend them. I just asked you to tell me one particular standard that you don't like. Can you give me an example of a bad standard?
>
> **BLOGGER:** I guess we will just have to agree to disagree. [ignoring the question]

Yes, the debater in me loves to probe. And the debater in me notices when poor thinking occurs. Even well-educated people often seem unable to make reasonable responses. In this case, I was left wondering what we were disagreeing about. We weren't even able to engage in a discussion that might have revealed points of contention!

I think you see the point. Students (and all of us) are bombarded with poor reasoning everywhere. My quest for real-life models of reasoning revealed evidence of more problems instead of examples of good thinking to share with students. I still had a long way to go in developing my reasoning-skills unit. I was pushed to continue by forces outside my classroom as well.

SO WHAT?

Kids say goofy things in class. TV shows are driven by ratings, and drama trumps reasoning. Why should we care? After all, teachers have nothing else to think about, right?

I understand. When I wrote *Well Spoken* (Stenhouse 2011), I had an uphill battle trying to persuade many others that we needed to address the poor oral communication that our students demonstrate every day. As I mentioned in that book, reader's theater is more effective if students speak well. Read-alouds are better, poetry recitations are better, explanations at the board are better, book reports are better, science fair project talks are better, research presentations are better, podcasts are better, class newscasts are better, foreign language dialogs are better, all discussions are better . . . Well, you get the idea. Virtually everything that happens in our classes is oral language dependent, and all of it is better if students are well spoken. Now it seems that more educators are on the bandwagon. I introduced a framework for understanding the components of all oral communication. Then I offered mini-lesson ideas that develop speaking skills and that every teacher can sneak into what they already do.

Indeed, this book is in part a response to *Well Spoken*. I spoke of the two parts of all oral communication: building the talk (everything you do *before you open your mouth*) and performing the talk (the things you do *as you are speaking*). We build talks designed to entertain and talks designed to inform. And as pointed out earlier, we often build talks designed to convince and persuade others. Those talks require good reasoning.

IT'S UP TO YOU

Do you ever have discussions in your class? Do you ever ask students to explain their thinking? Do you ask students to think about why something happened, whether in a novel, in Congress, or in a science lab? Do you have Socratic circles? Have you ever asked students to write a persuasive essay or give a persuasive speech? What other situations in your classes require reasoning skills? Reasoning may not have been a big part of our instruction, but now it needs to be addressed by all teachers at all grade levels. As we'll see in the next chapter, standards in every subject mention argument, claims, evidence, and more. That is only the immediate impetus for us, however. The standards came out of a desire to get all students ready for college and career, and both of those demand good thinking.

Teaching thinking will affect everything we do. By making small adjustments to what we already do, we can develop better thinking in all students. We can add little lessons that are practical and simple to implement and that will dramatically improve student thinking.

(Notice what just happened: I built an argument about why we should care about teaching reasoning skills. I talked about how *Well Spoken* made an argument for increasing oral communication instruction. I made an argument that with a small effort and a few tweaks, all of us can make a huge difference in students' thinking ability. See? Reasoning is everywhere, and the ability to reason well will be useful every day of our lives.)

WHERE WE'RE HEADED

Yes, I introduce terms that students haven't heard before. I talk about syllogisms, causal inference, and more. But then I take those terms and show how to translate them to your classroom. How did a teacher establish a Booger Patrol in her classroom and teach logic at the same time (Chapter 3)? How did a traveling debate become an opportunity for introducing ad hominem attacks (Chapter 8)? How does one teacher turn every "Well, duh!" comment into a chance to teach the structure of a good argument (Chapter 3)? We shall see, and in the process, we'll discover how to make some of the activities you already do become openings for improving student thinking.

What I hope to do in this book is take you through a series of steps that will lead students to habits of good thinking. Each chapter is organized in a similar way: I introduce a concept and offer definitions and explanations of key terms, I show a classroom example of a lesson, I offer several activities that can be used to help students learn the thinking, and I show some classroom vignettes with ideas from elementary and middle school teachers. Every chapter finishes with an argument in progress—showing where students should be after the instruction in that chapter.

Chapter 2 shares language from state standards. We'll see how thinking skills permeate every grade and every subject, and we'll see that the language of the standards is often confusing. I'll introduce some definitions to clear up that confusion and to guide our work in this book.

Chapter 3 introduces a basic building block of effective argument, the syllogism. We will see how that block can be used in all curricula, and we will learn how to teach students to create and use syllogisms.

Chapter 4 explains how students should analyze arguments. Is the argument well built? We will discover that it is possible to build a reasonable argument with false premises, so we will teach students to ask another question: are the statements in the argument true?

Chapter 5 shows how to teach students to provide support for their thinking—how to make sure that every statement has proof. We will teach students to provide evidence. By the end of Chapters 3, 4, and 5, students should be able to build strong arguments with support for every statement.

Chapter 6 moves us from logic and reasoning to persuasion. Statements of facts are seldom persuasive, so we will look at ways to move from cold arguments to hot persuasive writing and speaking. The art of rhetoric is introduced and made understandable for students. Chapter 6 also explains common persuasive tricks. Used in selling automobiles, candidates, soap, and homework, these tricks can be applied by students to get acceptance for their arguments.

Chapter 7 examines common reasoning errors. Quite often, student comments demonstrate errors of thinking. For example, we will look at a graph that seems, at first glance, to prove that the key to healthy marriages is eating less margarine. The example demonstrates one of a number of commonly made reasoning errors. Then we will look at other errors and share ways to teach students to avoid such mistakes.

Chapter 8 provides a collection of activities teachers have shared that have good thinking at their heart. We'll also look at some digital tools that teach or showcase argument and persuasion.

I don't suggest teaching a reasoning unit. Don't try to figure out how to make some big instructional change to your teaching. Instead, become aware of students' mistakes within the context of normal activities, and teach ways to help them avoid those mistakes in the future. The combined result of all the mini-lessons taught by you (and your teammates!) will be students with consistently good thinking.

CHAPTER 2

Thinking in the Standards

S tandards are certainly a hot-button topic as I write this, especially the Common Core State Standards. Indeed, as I noted in the previous chapter, we can find great examples for our argument and reasoning lessons by following the debate about those standards. All drama aside, the standards movement pushes us in some good directions. Updating instruction, emphasizing oral language, and increasing attention to reasoning skills are all changes that have come out of the standards movement. I notice that states not officially on board with the Common Core still believe in standards in general and still value much of what the Common Core espouses. I'll share some examples (primarily from the Common Core) to demonstrate how reasoning permeates all subjects and grade levels. Notice in Figure 2.1 how often *argument* or versions of that word show up in the guidelines.

FIGURE 2.1

Examples of Reasoning and Argumentation in Standards Documents

Common Core Reading: The reading standards focus on students' ability to read carefully and grasp information, arguments, ideas, and details based on evidence in the text. (See www.corestandards.org /other-resources/key-shifts-in-english-language-arts/.)

Common Core Writing: Although the standards still expect narrative writing throughout the grades, they also expect a command of sequence and detail that are essential for *effective argumentative* and informative writing. The standards' focus on *evidence-based writing* along with the ability to inform and *persuade* is a significant shift from current practice. (See www.corestandards.org/other-resources/key-shifts-in-english -language-arts/.)

Indiana Grade 7 Math: The standards expect students to make conjectures and *build a logical progression of statements* . . . justify their conclusions and communicate them to others . . . *reason inductively . . . making plausible arguments* . . . [Students] compare the effectiveness of two plausible *arguments* . . . *distinguish correct logic or reasoning.* (See http://www.doe.in.gov/sites/default/files/standards/mathematics/2014 -ias-mathematics-correlation-guide-grade-7-5-29-14.pdf.)

Common Core Speaking: The standards expect students to be able to evaluate a speaker's point of view, *reasoning, and use of evidence and rhetoric, assessing the stance, premises,* links among ideas, word choice, points of emphasis, and tone used. (See www.corestandards .org/ELA-Literacy/SL/11-12/.)

Indiana Academic Standards for Media Literacy: The standards expect students to *recognize claims in print, image, and multimedia and identify evidence used to support these claims.* (See www.doe.in.gov /sites/default/files/standards/enla/k-5_ela_draft-7-7-14-et.pdf, p. 34.)

As the examples in Figure 2.2 demonstrate, many standards expect young students, not just older ones, to begin developing strong and sophisticated reasoning and analytical skills.

FIGURE 2.2

Examples of Reasoning and Argumentation in Standards for Young Students

Common Core, Grade 1 <u>Writing</u>: The standards expect students to w*rite opinion pieces* in which they introduce the topic or name the book they are writing about, *state an opinion, supply a reason* for the opinion, and provide some sense of closure.

Common Core, Grade 1 <u>Writing</u>: The standards ask students to *write informative/explanatory texts* in which they *name a topic, supply some facts* about the topic, and provide some sense of closure.

Texas State Standards, <u>Grade 1 Reading</u>: The standards require students to *analyze, make inferences and draw conclusions* about expository text, and *provide evidence* from text to support their understanding (See http://ritter.tea.state.tx.us/rules/tac/chapter110 /ch110a.html#110.12.)

The previous examples apply primarily to language arts and math teachers. What about those who teach other subjects? Reasoning and argumentation show up often in their teaching guides as well. Examples from the Indiana state standards, shown in Figure 2.3, are typical of the requirements.

FIGURE 2.3

Examples of Reasoning and Argumentation in Standards Documents for Subjects Other than English and Math

Indiana State Standards, Grades 6–12 <u>History/Social Studies</u>: The standards expect students to *write arguments* focused on discipline-specific content. (See www.doe.in.gov/sites/default/files /standards/2014-04-15-contentlit-historysoc.pdf.)

Indiana State Standards, Grades 6–12 <u>Science/Technical Subjects</u>: The standards ask students to *write arguments* focused on discipline-specific content. (See www.doe.in.gov/sites/default/files /standards/2014-04-14-contentlit-sciencetech.pdf.)

Remember that standards are not creative. They are reactive to changes and demands in society and the global economy. They seek to set out the steps that will prepare students for life after school. Yes, we want students to master the standards but only because mastering them will be important beyond school. Good thinking is necessary for success in life.

THE BASICS

Argument. Reasoning. Claims. Logical progression of statements. Use of evidence. Rhetoric. The standards contain language with which we may be unfamiliar and that we may not be well prepared to teach. And of course, our plates are already full, yet we are being asked to do more. We are like the person at the all-you-can-eat buffet who has no chance of finishing everything on his plate but, even so, is being told to try the new entrée that just came out from the kitchen. Really, though, we already provide many activities that involve reasoning. All we need to do is tweak those activities to accomplish what we are being asked to do. I provide many lessons and activities in this book that, over time, will add up to good thinking by all students.

More troubling than the unfamiliarity of some of the words used in the standards is the lack of consistency in the language. One targeted skill has been given several different labels. The imprecision obscures the overlapping ideals. For example, teach argument *and* logical progression of statements? Actually, these are synonyms—teach one and you've got the other covered. It's unfortunate that the standards switch from one term to another, because the inconsistency confuses students as well as teachers. I railed against the shifting-language problem in *Well Spoken*. No two teachers had the same way of describing what it takes to be a great communicator. *Articulation, enunciation, elocution, clearly*—why so many words for one concept? I created a simpler way to understand and teach speaking skills. I found that a consistent language from class to class and grade to grade was valuable for students. The same principle—consistent language—applies to the teaching of thinking skills.

"Give reasons for your statement." "What premises lead to that conclusion?" "Do the reasons support the position?" "Do you have evidence for the claim, with warrants for the evidence and backing for the warrants?" These are questions teachers sent me when I asked online for prompts they used to elicit elaboration. In these examples, teachers have used different words to describe the same process. *Statement, conclusion, position,* and *claim* all describe the result of some train of thought; *reasons, premises,* and *warrants* all describe sentences used to lead us to that result.

Let's simplify things for ourselves and for our students. I have chosen this definition and use it throughout the book:

An argument *is a group of statements or premises that leads to a conclusion.*

I use *statements* and *premises* interchangeably—*statements* for younger students, *premises* for older students who may be interested in learning the language of logicians. I don't use the terms *warrant* or *claim* because I think they are not kid-friendly terms. I don't use the word *reason* in my definition because I think that word serves a different purpose, one that I explain in Chapter 6. If your school prefers a different definition, fine. Just be consistent with the language you choose, and ensure that the language is consistent from class to class within your school. We are really concerned with only one thing: good thinking.

The basis of good thinking? An argument. Of course, we have to change the way students think about the word *argument*. Let me repeat what I wrote in *Teaching the Core Skills of Listening & Speaking* (2014). Students think an argument is a fight of some sort, on a scale from bickering to a full-fledged shouting match. That is not how the word is used in the standards or how we will use it in this book. Share the definition I just highlighted with your students. Explain that an argument is a collection of sentences that have a special relationship with one another. They are designed to lead us to a conclusion, to prove something.

Of course, you could argue that this definition of argument is limiting. For example, you may have heard someone say, "Let me make the argument that students need more activity." By our definition of argument, however, the speaker should have said, "Let me offer the conclusion that students need more activity." Then, after hearing the conclusion, we could ask for the statements that led to it. Only then would we have an argument. That might seem to be a fine point and, perhaps, a picky one. Remember, though, that our goal as teachers is to make complexity clear, and using the same word in several different ways is confusing to students. An argument is a *group of statements*, not *one* statement.

Another caution: Teachers often say the words *argument and persuasion* together, as if the terms are synonymous. They are not. Although we usually make an argument to persuade someone to do something, we want to ensure that students know the words have different meanings. I use the words *cold* and *hot* to clarify the difference for my students. An argument is cold: it is made up of passionless sentences that lead us to a passionless conclusion. Persuasion is hot: it consists of tricks we use to make others care about that cold argument. The argument creates the product, but the persuasion and rhetoric sell the product. In the next chapter, we'll begin the process of building a good product.

ARGUMENT IN PROGRESS

High-stakes testing. Seems there is a never-ending discussion about its value, and as I write this, the new generation of tests is amplifying the debate. I am going to use that topic. It's a good topic, because reasonable arguments are available for proponents and opponents of testing. In my debate classes, we learned to build an argument for both sides of the proposition that was going to be debated. Indeed, we were required to toss a coin at some tournaments to see which side we would argue, so we had to prepare for both the affirmative and negative positions. For this book's example, I had to choose a side, so I tossed a coin. The result?

High-stakes testing is bad.

CHAPTER 3

That Seems Logical

How many of us took classes in logic when we were in school? Very few of us, I'd guess. If I suggest that all students should have lessons in logic, the immediate reaction will likely be, "No, I don't think that is appropriate for my students. For some older students and college kids, maybe, but logic would be way beyond my students." Let me suggest a different response. Logical thinking skills should not be thought of as necessary only for older students or highbrow smarty-pants and unavailable to the rest of us. We can make logic accessible to all students. Indeed, we *must* make it a priority to teach logic, because so many skills needed to do well in school (and in life) depend on logical thinking.

Think of discussions that occur in your classes. How well do students understand the need to build strong arguments? How well do they use logical thinking? I noticed in all of my classes that students tended to make discussion comments that were conclusions. They seldom explained the logical progression of ideas leading to the conclusion and infrequently offered evidence to support the ideas. It did not matter which topic, subject, or grade level. They were long on opinions and short on logical thinking. Here are some examples:

We should have less homework.
We should be allowed to have cell phones in school.
The United States should stay out of the conflict in Syria.
Stem cell research should be banned.
We should sell magazines instead of candy.

Brian, the main character in the book Hatchet, *will not survive the winter.*
I'm not going to need algebra in later life.
Marijuana is less dangerous than alcohol.
We need more recess.
Learning coding is a good idea.

All of those statements suggest the end of some train of thought, but how did the speakers get to the result? As teachers, we spend a lot of our time asking students to explain their thinking. A common prompt: "Can you give me reasons to support your statement?" Because all students are familiar with the words *reason* and *explain*, we rarely teach lessons about what we are really after. The words are actually tricky to understand. Let me give you an example.

GABBY: We should turn off lights when we leave the room.

TEACHER: Can you give me a reason?

GABBY: It's good for the environment.

Are we satisfied? The student gave a reason . . . or did she? There are many thinking steps between turning off classroom lights and saving the environment, so let's ask to hear them. *How* is a dark classroom helping the environment?

GABBY: We should turn off lights when we leave the room.

TEACHER: Give me three reasons to support your position.

GABBY: It's good for the environment. Lights use electricity. Making electricity pollutes the environment.

How about now? Did the student give us three reasons? Some would say yes, but I say no. Gabby offered two sentences to explain her one reason—good for the environment. In other words, she gave one good "reason" to turn off lights and an explanation about how lights affect the environment. One more example:

> **GABBY:** We should turn off lights when we leave the room.
>
> **TEACHER:** Give me three reasons to support your position.
>
> **GABBY:** It's good for the environment. It saves money. We don't need lights on when we aren't here.

Now we have three very different ideas. Is that what the teacher wanted when he told Gabby to give three reasons? I bet you have questions. Most teachers will ask Gabby for more elaboration. To students, such a request is puzzling:

> **TEACHER:** Can you explain those reasons?
>
> **GABBY:** You mean explain why I gave those reasons? I gave those reasons because I want us to turn off the lights.
>
> **TEACHER:** I mean give me the reason why you said it would be good for the environment.
>
> **GABBY:** Because you asked me to explain my position. That's the reason I said it.
>
> **TEACHER:** No, I mean how is turning off lights good for the environment?

Hmm. It seems that neither Gabby nor her teacher has a workable understanding of the words *reason* and *explain*. To make matters worse, some teachers reverse the use of those words.

> **GABBY:** We should turn off lights when we leave the room.
>
> **TEACHER:** Please explain your position.
>
> **GABBY:** It's good for the environment.
>
> **TEACHER:** Can you give me the reason you said that?
>
> **GABBY:** Because you asked me to explain my position. That's why I said it.

This conversation reminds me of the old "Who's on First" comedy routine of Abbott and Costello. Find it online if you haven't seen it. In that routine, baseball players have unusual names: the first baseman is named Who, and the second baseman is named What. Costello is trying to figure out the lineup.

"Who's on first?"
"Yes."
"Yes, what?"
"Who is on first."
"Don't ask me, I'm asking you!"

It *is* funny when we watch people circle around a solution that is obvious to the audience. But humor masks the seriousness of clarifying good thinking.

Let's clean up the language we use and expect students to use by being very specific, very consistent. What is really being asked? A student offered a conclusion: we should turn off the lights when we leave the classroom. "Give reasons" or "explain" means "tell me how you got to your conclusion." In other words (our words), what statements lead to that conclusion? When we ask for reasons or explanations, we are really asking for students to tell us the complete argument. Using the better, more specific term directs students to better responses. Consider this:

GABBY: We should turn off lights when we leave the room.

TEACHER: Interesting. That seems like the result of some line of thinking. What is your argument?

GABBY: When we leave lights on, it uses electricity. Electricity comes from a power plant. Power plants burn coal to make electricity. Burning coal causes air pollution. Air pollution causes global warming. So, we should turn off lights when we leave the room.

With unambiguous language, Gabby knows exactly what she needs to do. It is misleading to say, "Give me a reason"—that suggests that one

statement will suffice. It is misleading to say, "Give me three reasons"—
that implies either that we need three statements (Gabby needed five)
or that we want three different arguments (perhaps one about global
warming, one about cost savings for the district, and one about the sil-
liness of having lights on when no one is using them). "Explain how you
came up with that" or "Why do you say that?" or "What reasons do you
have for that?"—those are imprecise ways to prompt students to share
the complete argument. Ask instead for all the statements leading to
their conclusion.

THE BUILDING BLOCKS OF ALL ARGUMENT

We defined *argument* in Chapter 2, but how can we teach students to
build good arguments? One way is to introduce a logic lesson about the
syllogism, a building block for argument creation. Syllogism? A fancy
term, very highbrow! Not suitable for elementary or middle grades, at
least at first glance. Yet a syllogism is the most basic form of an argument. We offer premises that lead to an inescapable conclusion. Here
is the classic example (which I believe is in every logic book):

> *All men are mortal.*
> *Socrates is a man.*
> *Therefore Socrates is mortal.*

Notice the structure: two sentences that lead us to a final statement,
or two premises that force us to accept the conclusion. In formal logic,
the first statement is the major premise; the second is the minor premise; the third is the conclusion. Although we may not use that language
with younger students, the basic idea is easy to understand: statements
that force us to accept a conclusion. This is a simple concept to grasp
but often difficult to create.

There are three versions of syllogisms that are particularly common.
The Socrates syllogism fits this mold:

> *All [people/things] in a category are _____.*
> *This particular [person/thing] is in that category.*

Therefore, this [person/thing] is a _____.

For younger students, this may be the only type of syllogism to introduce. Older students may have fun with a second and third type:

Either A or B.
Not A.
Therefore B.

And

If A, then B.
A.
Therefore, B.

When I look at what I just wrote, it seems somehow unfriendly and un-fun, not at all useful for elementary or middle school students. Bear with me, though.

We use this logical structure all the time without realizing it. Think of faculty meetings at your school. I bet you can come up with several examples of syllogistic structure. The first type of syllogism was used in my school when we were discussing Kelly Gallagher's book *Readicide* and deciding how we could positively affect student reading.

All students should love reading.
Sustained reading of books chosen by the student leads to love of reading.
We should have sustained reading time every day.

We ended up putting a twenty-minute reading block into the schedule.

Another year, my school decided that teachers needed more instructional time with students. Our discussion about how to achieve it used the second type of syllogism:

We either lengthen the school day or shorten passing periods.

We can't lengthen the school day because of bus schedules.
Therefore, we have to shorten passing periods.

So we did. This led us to the third type of syllogism:

If we shorten passing periods, we will have a problem with tardy
 students.
We shortened passing periods.
We had a problem with tardies.

No one at the faculty meeting ever said, "I have a syllogism for that! If we shorten passing periods . . ." We were able to construct the arguments without specifically mentioning the form. Students benefit, though, if we teach them what happens behind the curtain and make them aware of the formal process.

If we teach students the structure of the syllogism, we can then teach them how to think backward from the conclusion they just expressed. "What was the thought process that made you think that?" "What statements would lead us to the conclusion?" Or, for upper grades, "What were the premises that led to that conclusion?" For most conclusions, there are many possibilities. Recall the statement "We should have less homework," for example. How could we have reached that conclusion? When students understand the structure of the basic building block, they can more easily respond to our request for an explanation of their thinking. They will come up with examples such as these:

Students don't learn well if they're tired.
Lots of homework keeps us up too late and makes us tired.
We should have less homework.

Studies show that all students need time to play.
Homework cuts the amount of playtime.
We should have less homework.

Teachers want to be liked by students.

Homework makes us dislike teachers.
We should have less homework.

Your class can probably come up with other possible arguments. Students create syllogisms in their heads and share the conclusions of those syllogisms without realizing what they have done. In other words, understanding this logical building block is not too advanced for our students; it is what they do all the time without being aware of it. Let's make that hidden thinking explicit. Don't shy away from using the term *syllogism*, by the way. I have found that students are able to grasp the terminology and are inspired to learn more when I share "advanced" language with them.

Students will come up with ideas for different building blocks in addition to the three we have shown. When we share "If A, then B . . . ," students will likely ask, "Could we do 'If *not* A, then B'?" Yep.

If it does not rain, we will go outside.
It is not raining.
Yay! Let's go!

We want to encourage students to think in this way, to come up with different ways to build a logical argument. The key concept: understanding that statements do not stand alone but must be put together to build an argument.

IN PRACTICE

Sandy Otto is an exceptional teacher in Minnesota. She spent many years teaching fifth grade before moving to middle school, where she teaches English. After reading some books by Kelly Gallagher, her "edu-hero," she became committed to generating deeper thinking about texts. Pursuing that goal, Sandy attended a workshop about Socratic seminars and decided that giving students power in discussions and providing deep, enriching texts for those discussions would be important steps in the process. Sandy started collecting interesting, multifaceted readings about various topics. Now she uses those readings in Socratic seminars once a week.

Sandy noticed, however, that her students were still very literal in their thinking. They could find the "right there" answers, but they struggled to extend the ideas of the texts. She decided to teach them the "ACE" strategy: Answer, Cite, Extend. Students knew that to "extend," they had to make inferences and connections. They also had to evaluate the ideas presented and form their own opinions. Students had no trouble coming up with opinions, but they had a hard time explaining them. Phrased differently, they had conclusions but had difficulty with the statements that led to those conclusions. The problems were in the realm of argument and reasoning. Sandy wanted to help them but didn't quite know which skills were needed, let alone how to teach them. She sought help in the Twitterverse, and we connected. She began applying the ideas in this book. We'll visit her class often to watch her lead students to better thinking.

Here's how Sandy helps her students develop competence with syllogisms. First, she shares the definition of the word *syllogism* and explains its importance for developing good arguments. She also shares the structure of the three types of syllogisms that we noted previously. Next, Sandy hands out a Syllogism Sort activity (Figure 3.1). Students cut the paper into sections and then work in small groups to categorize the examples. For example, the students will see that the "wind chill" argument is an "If A, then B" type of syllogism, and the "robin" argument is an "All A are B" type.

FIGURE 3.1

Syllogism Sort Activity

If the wind chill is −40 degrees this morning, there will be a snow day. The wind chill is −40 degrees. There is a snow day.	We either see a movie or go to the mall. There are no good movies playing. Let's go to the mall.
We can work either in partners or individually. There is nobody I want to work with. I'll work by myself.	If I don't study for my math test, I might fail. I didn't study for the test. I just might fail.
If I spend all my money, I'll be broke. I spent all my money. Darn. Now I'm broke.	All birds have wings. A robin is a bird. Therefore, a robin has wings.
All amphibians have webbed feet. Frogs have webbed feet. Therefore, frogs are amphibians.	I can drive to school or ride the bus. My car won't start. I guess I'll take the bus.
No human is perfect. I am a human. Therefore, I'm not perfect.	If you win the race, you get a trophy. I have a trophy. I must have won the race.
You either wear your seat belt or you don't ride in my car. You won't wear a seat belt. Then you won't be riding in my car.	All teachers have students. Mrs. Otto is a teacher. She must have students.
If you finish all your dinner, you can have dessert. You finished all your dinner. Here's your dessert.	Either the Minnesota Twins or the Detroit Tigers will win the game. The Tigers lost. That means the Twins won the game.
Tweets must not exceed 140 characters. This is a tweet. Therefore, it will be 140 characters or less.	All historical fiction is set in the past. This story is set in 1975. Therefore, it must be historical fiction.

Once students become more familiar with the structure of good building blocks, Sandy hands out the activity shown in Figure 3.2, and has students come up with the statements that would lead to the suggested conclusion.

FIGURE 3.2

Creating Statements to Support Conclusions

	Example:
_____ _____ **Students should have less homework.**	Students don't learn well if they're tired. Lots of homework keeps students up late. **Students should have less homework.**
_____ _____ **We should be allowed to have cell phones in school.**	_____ _____ **Students should be able to chew gum in school.**
_____ _____ **Everyone should learn a second language.**	_____ _____ **More parks should be built in the city.**
_____ _____ **High schools should start later than elementary schools.**	_____ _____ **Using PVLEGS (poise, voice, life, eye contact, gestures, speed) is important when speaking.**

With that preparation, she moves to application of the ideas in an authentic project. Sandy's school has lockers, but students are not allowed to have locks. Needless to say, some students think this is an odd restriction. When Sandy asks students for their opinions, she gets statements of conclusions, which she displays on the board:

We should totally be allowed to have locks.
Not allowing locks is dumb.
We can be trusted with locks.

But not all students favor locks. Some make comments such as these:

Having a lock would slow me down.
Too many kids will have problems with locks.

Having taught her students about syllogisms, Sandy can now ask students to work backward from those statements of conclusions. She selects one statement and models filling out the argument with the class.

> **SANDY:** Let's build an argument for the first one. What would lead someone to believe that we should totally be allowed to have locks?
>
> **BRAYDEN:** We have valuable stuff! I don't want someone taking it or messing with it.
>
> **SHANIA:** Someone took my calculator once! Brayden's right.
>
> **SANDY:** Good! We have one premise: students have valuable things. So? So what? We are missing a premise, aren't we?
>
> **CHARISSE:** If we had locks, no one could take those things. It's obvious!
>
> **SANDY:** Maybe, but it is our job to be sure the arguments we make are obvious. Let's look at what we have. [She writes on the board.]
>
> > *Students have valuable things.*
> > *Locks keep valuable things from being taken.*
> > *Therefore, we should totally be allowed to have locks.*
>
> **SANDY:** Have we done it? Is that a logical argument? Do we need the word *totally*? Well, that's a different lesson, isn't it? With a partner, come up with some other logical argument. I bet you can think of several ways to get us to that conclusion.

After some discussion time, she challenges the pairs to come up with the statements that would support *not* having locks, perhaps supporting the idea that too many kids will have problems. (For example, "Students are forgetful. Locks require keys or remembering combinations. Therefore, kids will have problems.") At the end of the partner time, each student creates his or her own argument on the topic. They may use ideas from the class time, but they are free to come up with new ideas as well. The only requirement is to build the arguments with the proper form.

BIGGER BUILDING BLOCKS

You probably have thought that two statements may not be sufficient to accomplish every purpose. My school served french fries in the lunchroom. Many students spent all of their lunch money on fries and bought nothing else. It occurred to some teachers that perhaps the school was encouraging poor eating habits and that fries should not be sold. It turned out that our cafeteria was a separate entity in the district, responsible for generating its own revenue. French fries were a big moneymaker. The cafeteria managers offered an argument that fit the classic three-line style:

We can continue to provide lunch service only if we make money.
French fries generate money.
We need to sell fries.

Our argument wasn't so tidy.

French fries contain lots of fat and calories.
Fat and calories lead to obesity.
Childhood obesity is a growing problem.
By offering fattening foods, we are contributing to childhood obesity.
We have to stop selling fries.

Four premises leading to a conclusion? Is that okay? Yes. A professor of logic might point out that four premises do not represent a syllogism. Teachers of adolescents should not be purists. Many arguments require additional steps.

Think of Legos. You've seen the size choices. My children and I called them the "one-dot Lego," the "two-dot Lego," the "four-dot Lego," and so on. Some things could be built with the smallest Lego; some things required bigger sizes. Have students think of arguments that way.

Gabby needed a five-dot Lego, a five-premise "syllogism," if you will, to build her Turn Off the Lights argument.

THE HIDDEN ARGUMENT

My poor dad. He was hit with two syllogisms in the story I told at the beginning of this book. Now you can probably see them:

No one wants to be sexist.
Suggesting that taking out the garbage is a "boy's job" is sexist.
Don't ask me to take out the garbage.

Exercise is good for health.
Taking out garbage is a type of exercise.
You should take out the garbage.

I'm guessing that although you knew I was trying to get out of some work, you didn't notice that I had used the logical building block we have been discussing in this chapter. Most often, the argument is not specifically laid out in a recognizable form. Once we get students into the habit of logical thinking, they will see syllogisms everywhere. Then we can ask them to see the implied syllogisms that are common in reading and in speech. As I mentioned when discussing our faculty meeting, no one specifically said, "Here is a syllogism to prove my point!" To be sure, it can be tricky to find the argument hidden in the expression of it.

Sometimes, the statements aren't in order. My wife was at the city of Aurora courthouse for jury duty as I wrote this. Now you know where we live—Aurora. Do you recognize the argument you used to figure that out?

Only residents of a city get jury duty in that city.
Erik's wife has jury duty in Aurora.
The Palmers live in Aurora.

Often students will have to look closely and rearrange sentences to understand the train of thought.

Sometimes, a key premise is unstated. You noticed that often a premise states the obvious. Socrates is a man. Did we need to say that? We all know that. Or think of Sandy's class. A student may have said, "We have valuable things, so we gotta have locks." Everyone knows that locks protect things, so that statement was never made. It was there, though.

We have valuable things.
(Locks protect valuable things.)
We should have locks.

Student discussions are full of implied premises: statements that assume we all know and agree about some ideas. For example, Sandy asked me to participate in a classroom discussion via Skype. Students were discussing the "Butterfly Struggle" story. There are several versions of the story, but the original author is not known. Most versions describe a young person watching a butterfly struggling to break out of its cocoon. A wise person tells the child not to interfere. Unfortunately, the child can't resist helping, and the butterfly falls to the ground, unable to fly. According to the story, opening the cocoon for the butterfly kept the wings from developing needed strength, which would have come had it been left to struggle. The essence of the story is that struggle is a good thing, and students seemed to agree.

If I don't make mistakes, I won't learn.
We need struggles or else we'll be spoiled rotten.
Without struggles, we wouldn't have our stuff. People have struggled to give us our stuff.
Yeah, what if Columbus had stayed home to watch Netflix?
Struggles make life worthwhile; otherwise it's boring.
Entertainment is based on struggle.
Watching struggle is sad!
What if you ask for help? Should I say no?

Many of these are syllogisms with implied, understood, and agreed-upon statements. I've underlined the premise that was unstated. In some cases, both premises are implied.

Learning is good.
We learn from mistakes.
If I don't make mistakes, I won't learn.

Being spoiled is bad.
Struggles keep us from being spoiled.
We need struggles.

Having stuff is good.
Our stuff comes from people who have struggled.
Struggling is good.

A boring life would be bad.
Struggles keep things from being boring.
Struggles make life worthwhile.

YOUR STUDENTS, YOUR CLASS

I don't advocate teaching the previous concepts as part of a logic unit. Instead, embed little lessons within other units that you regularly teach. Don't feel that you must teach everything included in this chapter all at once. Indeed, you don't need to teach everything included in this chapter. You know your students and their needs. And you know that all students need to be able to construct and recognize good arguments. As you prepare them for a book discussion, for example, share the form of a syllogism and ask them to make "form"al arguments to explain what they think the main character will do next. As you discuss lab safety or hallway behavior, ask students to build the arguments behind the rules. As you teach the Constitutional Convention, look for the statements used that favored a strong central government and those that led to favoring states' rights. Once you start looking, you'll see arguments everywhere. All of them are opportunities to teach good thinking.

IDEAS IN ACTION: STUDENT-GENERATED SYLLOGISMS

It is not hard for students to create their own examples of syllogisms. Share the form of a logical argument and ask them to come up with ideas from current units of study.

A kindergarten teacher can demonstrate good arguments without teaching logic:

All days have twenty-four hours.
Today, Tuesday, is a day, isn't it? So how many hours does it have?
Class: Twenty-four!

If we eat a lot of candy, we get sick.
Brown Bear ate a lot of candy. What do think will happen to him?
Class: He'll get sick!

As appropriate, teachers in grades 1 and beyond can begin explaining the thinking students have been exposed to in kindergarten. An elementary teacher working on photosynthesis may lead students to come up with these:

All plants need sunlight for photosynthesis.
Seaweed is a plant.
Therefore, seaweed needs sunlight.

All people need oxygen to live.
Plants produce oxygen.
Therefore, people need plants.

All fruits have seeds.
Though some people think a tomato is a vegetable, a tomato has
*   seeds.*
They are wrong! It is a fruit!

Math teachers:

All figures with four sides are quadrilaterals.
A trapezoid has four sides.
Trapezoids are quadrilaterals.

The sponsor of the student council can also get involved.

We can sell either magazines or wrapping paper.
The pep squad already sells wrapping paper.
We have to sell magazines.

Every teacher has probably offered an opportunity for students to create this one:

If I pass all the quizzes, I don't have to take the final test.
I passed the quizzes.
Woot woot! No final!

Look for places where students can generate syllogisms. They are everywhere. We will discuss in Chapter 5 how to decide which argument is best and how to support the premises. Here, we just want to help students see how logical thinking works. We want students to get into the habit of thinking about syllogisms and looking for them every time they see or hear conclusions, every time they write or speak.

IDEAS IN ACTION: ASK BETTER QUESTIONS

A teacher finds an article about the need to increase activity for desk-bound workers. The article discusses health benefits of small changes such as working at a stand-up desk. Students read the article and are given these questions:

1. How can you increase the number of calories you burn in a day?
2. Do you find the argument in this piece compelling?
3. Select a passage and respond to it.

Pretty classic stuff, right? A comprehension check, an opinion option, and a writing prompt. Better questions would greatly improve this reading activity and give us a way to reinforce building arguments. I'll assume that reading teachers want to include comprehension checks, so I suppose Question One is necessary to see whether a student can find "right there" information. I take issue with Question Two. Before you ask students whether they find an argument compelling, let's ask whether they can tell us what the argument is! How about this:

2. What is the author's argument? What conclusion is offered, and what statements lead us to that conclusion?

The article probably suggested this argument:

Inactivity causes health problems.
Office and school work is sedentary and inactive.
Offices and schools should make changes to increase activity during the day.

Once the argument is laid out, we could continue with this (which is getting ahead of ourselves a bit by including Chapter 5 information):

3. Is there evidence for each statement?

If we don't want to focus on that yet, a better Question Three would be this one:

3. Select a statement in the argument and respond to it.

Spending a little time crafting better questions will lead to better understanding of argumentative writing and more focused student writing.

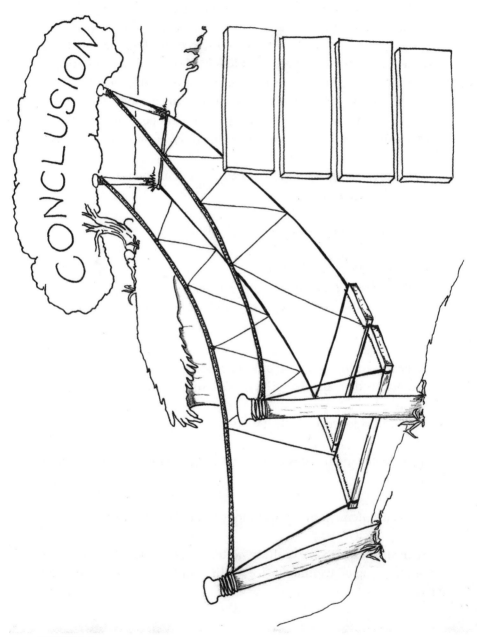

FIGURE 3.3
Graphic Organizer for Building an Argument

IDEAS IN ACTION: A VISUAL AID FOR BUILDING AN ARGUMENT

Give students a visual way to see the need for developing an argument. Figure 3.3 uses a bridge analogy, and it makes clear to students that we have to build a way to get to the conclusion. Gabby wants us to turn off the lights. Her goal is to get us to accept that conclusion, but we don't have any way to get there unless she finishes the bridge.

IDEAS IN ACTION: FIND HIDDEN ARGUMENTS

Collect (or have students collect) examples of arguments that are hidden in text or in speech. Challenge students to piece the arguments together into a logical form. Even casually overheard comments can be used:

> *"Man, am I hungry."*
> *"Did you eat all of your lunch?"*
> *"No."*
> *"Well, duh!"*

Turns out that every "Well, duh" comment is a syllogism in disguise.

> *If you don't finish lunch, you will be hungry.*
> *You didn't finish lunch.*
> *Well, duh, you're hungry.*

You didn't study and you got a bad grade? Well, duh. You got grounded because you got home late? Well, duh. Look for small opportunities like this to reinforce good thinking all year long. Advanced students will find examples, too, once you tell them to be on the lookout. "Sonya must have gotten all As because her parents have a bumper sticker on their car, and only kids on honor roll get that bumper sticker." Remember: We don't have to drop what we do and add a new unit on logic. We just have to use opportunities that arise during our normal day to reinforce reasoning skills.

APPLICATION IN DAILY PROCEDURES

As I mentioned, my wife, Anne, teaches fourth grade. One day she came home and told me that she was grossed out by the number of kids in her class who . . . how to put this nicely . . . um . . . well . . . picked their noses. And apparently the students did not feel the need to get tissues because the bottom of the desk was so convenient. Anne took action and created Booger Patrol. Now, once a week (more often in cold season), she stops everything, has students take everything off their desks, hands out antibacterial wipes, and insists that they wipe every surface, top and bottom. Inevitably, one student will ask, "Why do we have to do this?" The temptation is to say, "Because your desks are gross!" but instead Anne treats the question as an opportunity for a logic lesson:

ANNE: I've concluded that it's time for Booger Patrol. How do you suppose I came to think that?

STUDENT: Because our desks are dirty!

ANNE: True, but I call it Booger Patrol for a reason, so can you be more specific?

STUDENT: 'Cause some people wipe their noses on their hands and then their hands are on the desk.

STUDENT: I saw someone pick his nose and wipe it on the bottom of the desk.

STUDENT: Gross! It's not from me! Who sits at my desk during math?

ANNE: I'm not saying it's any one person's fault. But so what if someone wipes their nose on their hand? Is that bad?

STUDENT: It has germs! We could get their germs! Yuck.

ANNE: So what we're saying is this [she writes on the board]:

Some people are putting germs on desks.
Germs are bad and can cause colds.
Therefore, we should clean the desks.

Does that answer the question "Why do we have to do this?"

APPLICATION IN LISTENING

Create an organizer for students to use as they listen to media commentators. Figure 3.4 shows an example. Caution students that they will not necessarily fill the rows in order. It is likely that they will hear a conclusion first.

FIGURE 3.4
Graphic Organizer for Listing Examples of Premises Heard in Speech

Premise 1	
Premise 2	
Premise 3 (if needed)	
Premise 4 (if needed)	
Premise 5 (if needed)	
Conclusion	

APPLICATION IN VOCABULARY

This is a great activity to use before starting a new content-area lesson or topic. First, choose twenty to twenty-five key vocabulary words from the material to be studied and present the list to your students. For example, in a unit about biomes, *niche, producer, consumer, adaptation, climate, coniferous forest,* and *tundra* might show up. Ask the students to work together in small groups to determine five categories for the vocabulary words. Students might say that some words fall into a category called "animals" and some fit into a category called "plants," and so on. Students put the words on sticky notes and place each one in the category where they think it best fits. Students must build arguments to support their category choices and word placement. Once decisions have been made and all words have been placed on large pieces of chart paper, the groups can choose titles for their charts. Each small group should present its chart to the class and be prepared to explain the reasoning behind the choices.

APPLICATION IN MATH

When I taught sixth-grade math, I assigned a Problem of the Week. On Mondays, I would hand out a difficult problem, and the students had until Friday to solve it. They could struggle with it for a week or ask others or research or do whatever they wanted to come up with a solution. All I wanted was an explanation in writing of the thinking behind that solution. We can use the Problem of the Week to reinforce our teaching of the syllogism:

> Three students walk into a bakery. The owner says, "Do all three of you want a doughnut?" The first student says, "I don't know." The second student says, "I don't know." The third student says, "Yes!" How did the third student come up with his answer?

A possible explanation: The answer to the store owner's question would be "Yes" only if all three students wanted a doughnut. Each would have to want a doughnut; otherwise, "Do all three of you want a doughnut?" would be answered, "No, only two of us do" or "No, only one of us does" or "No, none of us do." Student Three had to think logically.

"If Student One didn't want a doughnut, he could have answered 'No.' He would have thought, I *don't want a doughnut, so therefore, it isn't true that* all *of us want a doughnut*. So I figured Student One must want a doughnut. The thing is, he didn't know whether *we* wanted doughnuts, so he couldn't speak for us and say, 'Yes, all of us want doughnuts.' If Student Two didn't want a doughnut, he could have answered 'No,' but he didn't, so he must want a doughnut, too. He couldn't say 'Yes' because he didn't know if *I* wanted one. Therefore, both Students One and Two want doughnuts, and I want a doughnut, so I say 'Yes!'" Writing it as a syllogism would look like this:

> *If a student says "No" to the store owner, he doesn't want a doughnut.*
> *Students One and Two did not say "No."*
> *Students One and Two want doughnuts!*

ARGUMENT IN PROGRESS

So where does the discussion in this chapter leave the high-stakes testing argument I introduced in Chapter 2? Initially, we had only a conclusion. Now we know that the conclusion must have been based on some train of thought. We could probably invent a number of ways to get to the conclusion, but I've chosen this route for now (argument changes are italicized):

> *Students need lots of instructional time to master important skills.*
> *Testing takes away from direct instruction.*
> High-stakes testing is bad.

CHAPTER 4

Evaluating Arguments

Now that students are proficient with the building blocks of argument, we have to teach them how to evaluate the arguments they build. A child starts playing with Legos by understanding the pieces and how they fit together. Some of the early creations are, well, just assembled blocks. At some point (and if parents have enough money!), the child might make something impressive with the blocks. So it is with premises and conclusions. Early creations are just blocks put together. How do we make sure the result is impressive? Start by sharing the three important questions that follow.

ARE THERE DIFFERENT WAYS TO GET TO THE CONCLUSION?

Here is a Twitter conversation I had with a teacher:

> **ME**: I'm looking for help with a new book. Anyone teach reasoning skills and want to share ideas?
>
> **TEACHER**: Sure. I have students take a topic from *Time* magazine and take a position.
>
> **ME**: Sounds like a good activity. How do you teach them how to take a position?
>
> **TEACHER**: I require them to state a position and give three STRONG reasons.
>
> **ME**: How do you teach them what a STRONG reason is?

The conversation ended there. First, as we discussed in the previous chapter, her language is confusing. Did she want one conclusion (position?) with three premises (reasons?) in the argument, or did she want one conclusion with three different ways to get to that conclusion? Second, I suspect the chat ended because she didn't have any lessons about strength of reasons. We do this a lot with students—asking them to provide something without teaching them how to do so.

In addition to showing students how to build arguments, we must let them practice and evaluate the quality of various expressions of logical thinking. What makes one argument better than another? Encourage students to build to a conclusion in several different ways, and then deconstruct the methods before determining the most successful. Students need to be able to see many different ways to get to a desired result so that they will be able to have options when it comes time to select an argument to persuade.

Any math teacher can tell you there are a number of ways to get to a result. If the answer is 14, that could be the result of $10 + 4$ or $7 + 7$ or 7×2 or $27 - 13$ and so on. Similarly, there are often many possible ways to build to a certain conclusion. Think back to students' arguments that supported getting rid of homework. They all successfully led to the conclusion, but you probably thought one argument was weaker than the others. We will probably not modify our homework policies based on a desire to be well liked. It is imperative that we introduce students to the idea that some arguments are better than others. I talk much more about how to identify the most persuasive arguments in Chapter 7, but here I want to introduce the notion that some logically valid and actually true arguments can be weak. If you recall, I tried two ways to get my father to release me from garbage duty. Both arguments were well constructed, but neither was successful. Still, I believe to this day that I could have crafted an argument to persuade my dad to have someone else take out the trash. I just didn't come up with it at the time.

DOES IT ADD UP?

A logician asks, "Is the argument valid?" In the world of logic, an argument is valid if the statements lead to the conclusion. To say an argument is valid is not the same as saying, "I agree with the conclusion." It refers only to whether the structure of the argument is correct or not. I ask students to think of these as math problems: Does it add up? We aren't discussing right/wrong, support/lack of support, or agree/disagree yet. All I want students to do at this point is think, *If the statements were true, would it force us to accept the conclusion?* Think back to the famous example:

All men are mortal.
Socrates is a man.
Socrates is mortal.

The argument clearly adds up. There is no way out. If men are mortal, and if Socrates is a man, we have to accept that he is mortal.

But let's parse this point. Here is a *valid* argument:

All teachers are purple.
Mr. Palmer is a teacher.
Therefore, Mr. Palmer is purple.

I'm not purple. This argument is obviously wrong. It starts with an incorrect premise: it isn't true that all teachers are purple. Yet the argument is still *valid*. Why? Because it adds up, and that is all we want right now. *If* all teachers are purple, and *if* Mr. Palmer is a teacher, then it would have to be true that he is purple. Remember, all we want students to do at this point is be able to see if statements lead to a conclusion.

This line of thought might seem to be beyond the grasp of young students. They may not be able to understand the difference between *correct* or *true* and *valid*. Older students tend to find the idea quite intriguing and enjoy the mind-blowing aspect of having to admit that a purple Mr. Palmer argument is actually allowable in logic. Students at every age need to know that there is no point in elaborating on an argument—finding evidence, explaining statements—if it never adds up in the first place. Let's look at some examples:

All students who go to Campus Middle School take P.E.
Kim, a seventh grader, does not go to Campus Middle School.
Therefore, Kim doesn't take P.E.

Both statements are true . . . but we don't care about that at the moment. By using true statements, though, we avoid giving students a different way to challenge the argument. Remember, all we want to know now is whether the statements force us to accept the conclusion. In this case, however, there is something wrong with the argument. Students will spend some time thinking about it before they figure out the problem: to say that *all students* who go to Campus Middle School take physical education does not mean that *only students* who go to Campus Middle School have P.E. classes. Indeed, you probably have P.E. classes at your school.

How about this example?

If you practice the violin, you can be in the school orchestra.
Dave does not practice the violin.
Dave can't be in the orchestra.

Again, to make it clear to students that we are interested only in the "math" of the argument, both statements are correct. Your students will be quick to see the issue: couldn't Dave play the viola or trumpet or oboe and get into the orchestra?

One more example:

Every American believes in freedom.
Iranians are not American.
Iranians don't believe in freedom.

We can see the problem. It is the same type of fallacy—*all* does not equal *only*—shown in the example featuring Campus Middle School and P.E. In spite of its invalidity, I have heard this argument on a prominent news channel. We absolutely want students to be able to create good arguments, but we also want them to analyze arguments they see and hear. Let's not lose sight of the idea that as they become better thinkers themselves, they are also becoming better at evaluating the thinking of others, an important life skill.

Advanced students will be interested to see that an argument can have true statements yet be invalid. This notion impressed me when I read about it in my college logic book (Salmon 1963).

All mammals have hearts.
A dog has a heart.
Therefore, a dog is a mammal.

That argument looks correct. All three statements are true, but that isn't our interest yet. The question is, do the two premises lead us to the conclusion? This example gives us a chance to test a strategy for determining validity: change a word. Make a substitution for a key term:

All mammals have hearts.
A frog has a heart.
Therefore, a frog is a mammal.

Oops. We were led to a wrong conclusion, so something must be wrong in the way we set up the argument. We have seen the problem before—the first statement didn't say *only* mammals have hearts. This reveals an important point: every word matters. Again, this is advanced thinking for students, but some of your students will love playing around with good-looking yet invalid arguments.

Before students spend time finding evidence to support an argument or trying to write a persuasive piece, make sure they know how to build a strong core argument.

IS THAT RIGHT?

Let's leave the realm of the logician and get to what I think is a more comfortable place for most of us. Purple Mr. Palmer? Obviously, this is wrong. Only a logician would try to pretend that such an argument is OK. We don't have many occasions in life when we try to convince others about something as dumb as purple teachers. We want students to start with the right structure, but we also want them to make meaningful points. We need to spend most of our time, then, discussing other ways to evaluate arguments.

The quickest response we have to statements we hear is probably "Yeah, that's right!" or "Nope, that isn't right!" So our job just got a little harder: we have to build carefully, *and* we have to use the correct materials. The "purple Palmer" argument is well built, but the materials are quite suspect.

Students will not have a hard time figuring out what it means to evaluate the *truth* of an argument. Every student will agree that "purple Palmer" is built with wrong statements. Students will easily understand that all of the premises/reasons/statements in a "good" argument must be statements of truth. Look at examples we have used previously.

If you don't finish lunch, you will be hungry.
You didn't finish lunch.
Well, duh, you're hungry.

All figures with four sides are quadrilaterals.
A trapezoid has four sides.
All trapezoids are quadrilaterals.

We have valuable things.
Locks protect valuable things.
We should have locks.

All of these add up. All of them are made with statements that wouldn't generate much disagreement. It is often tricky to judge the truth of the statements in an argument, however. What about these?

Ice caps are needed to moderate temperatures on Earth.
Carbon dioxide emissions are causing ice caps to melt.
Most of the carbon dioxide emissions are from human activities.
*We have to pass laws to limit the human activities that emit carbon
    dioxide.*

We should teach only important skills.
Spelling is not an important skill in the twenty-first century.
Stop teaching spelling.

The arguments seem well built, but are the premises true? In these examples, I think most people will agree with the first statement in each set, but many will dispute the second statements. That will lead us to the job of proving every statement, which we'll discuss in the next chapter.

IN PRACTICE
Sandy's students have been introduced to logical thinking and have had some time to practice constructing logical arguments through specific activities and informal discussions. She focused on the *form* of a well-built argument, not the *content*. Now she presents PowerPoint slides in class with the two ways to test a syllogism: Does it add up? Is each statement true? She leads a class discussion, using Figure 4.1 as a prompt she posts on her whiteboard.

FIGURE 4.1

Testing Syllogisms

Directions: In the right-hand column, identify any problems with the premises shown in the left-hand column.	
All clocks have hands. I have hands. Therefore, I am a clock.	
All teachers are purple. Mr. Palmer is a teacher. Therefore, Mr. Palmer is purple.	
All students at Woodland take P.E. Jake doesn't go to Woodland. Therefore, Jake doesn't take P.E.	
If you play violin, you can be in the school orchestra. Erin plays the cello. Therefore, Erin can't be in the school orchestra.	
All mammals have hearts. A frog has a heart. Therefore, a frog is a mammal.	
Every American believes in freedom. Italians are not Americans. Therefore, Italians don't believe in freedom.	
All combs have teeth. I have teeth. Therefore, I must be a comb.	
If you're in Mrs. Otto's class, you attend Woodland. Troy is not in Mrs. Otto's class. Therefore, he does not attend Woodland.	

* class collaboration

Look at the following syllogisms. They are all valid arguments but are untrue. Analyze what makes them untrue.

multi-meaning word

All clocks have hands. I have hands. ✔ Therefore, I am a clock.	*wrong kind of* ⊙ *My hand*
All teachers are purple. ✔ Mr. Palmer is a teacher. Therefore, Mr. Palmer is purple.	*not all teachers are purple*
All students at Woodland take P.E. Jake doesn't go to Woodland. Therefore, Jake doesn't take P.E. ✔	*another school could also have P.E.*
If you play violin, you can be in the school orchestra. ✔ Erin plays the cello. So Erin can't be in the school orchestra.	*other string instruments (like cellos) could be in the orchestra, too*
All mammals have hearts. ✔ A frog has a heart. Therefore, a frog is a mammal.	*not only mammals have hearts*
Every American believes in freedom. ✔ Italians are not Americans. Therefore, Italians don't believe in freedom.	*it's not only Americans who believe in freedom*
All combs have teeth. I have teeth. ✔ Therefore, I must be a comb.	*comb mouth (like hand one) different kind of teeth*
If you're in Mrs. Otto's class, you attend Woodland. Troy is not in Mrs. Otto's class. Therefore, he does not attend Woodland. ✔	*more than one teacher works at Woodland*

FIGURE 4.2

"Testing Syllogisms" filled in after class discussion

Sandy tells her students that each example has a problem. Students raise hands to share their ideas about which problem occurred. You can see the results of their thinking by looking at the notes Sandy took (see Figure 4.2).

Students begin to understand how to look for errors in argument construction. Sandy challenges her students to look for arguments in everyday life and return to class with examples. She tells them this will be an ongoing assignment, not nightly homework. Any time they hear or see an interesting argument, they should bring it into class for examination.

IDEAS IN ACTION: PLAY WITH MATH

As I was learning addition, my teacher gave me lots of practice problems:

$$5 + 2 = \underline{\hspace{1cm}} \qquad 8 + 6 = \underline{\hspace{1cm}} \qquad 9 + 9 = \underline{\hspace{1cm}}$$

Then the problems got trickier:

$$5 + \underline{\hspace{1cm}} = 7 \qquad \underline{\hspace{1cm}} + 6 = 14 \qquad 9 + \underline{\hspace{1cm}} = 18$$

Use the same kind of thinking to practice argument building. Sandy created the exercises shown in Figure 4.3 for her class. Notice that she sometimes asks students to provide statements and sometimes to make the conclusion from statements.

FIGURE 4.3

Building Arguments

Directions: Some examples ask you to create statements to support the conclusion, whereas others ask you to create a conclusion based on the statements provided.	
All herbivores eat only plants. _____ . A moose is an herbivore.	If I don't comb my hair before bed, it is all tangled in the morning. _____ . My hair was all tangled this morning.
_____ The dog didn't bark. The thief must have been someone the dog knew.	Drinking lots of water keeps you hydrated. I drink lots of water. _____ .
Sneezing without covering my mouth spreads germs. I sneezed without covering my mouth. _____ .	_____ . Subway was out of flatbread. Therefore, I had my sandwich on wheat bread.
I'll wear either a sweater or sweatshirt. _____ Therefore, I will wear a sweatshirt.	All books on the top shelf are half off. _____ . Therefore, it is half off.
_____ It froze last night after the rain stopped. Therefore, the roads were icy.	If I read twenty minutes each day, I will increase my vocabulary. I read twenty minutes each day. _____ .
I take either the freeway or the back roads to get to work. There was a huge accident on the freeway. _____ .	All students who learn to communicate effectively will be more successful. _____ . Therefore, I will be more successful.

APPLICATION IN READING

Find the Sherlock Holmes mystery "The Adventure of the Blue Carbuncle." In that short story, Sherlock picks up a hat and tells Watson about its owner:

> That the man was highly intellectual is of course obvious upon the face of it, and also that he was fairly well-to-do within the last three years, although he has now fallen upon evil days. He had foresight, but has less now than formerly, pointing to a moral retrogression, which, when taken with the decline of his fortunes, seems to indicate some evil influence, probably drink, at work upon him. This may account also for the obvious fact that his wife has ceased to love him . . . He has, however, retained some degree of self-respect . . . He is a man who leads a sedentary life, goes out little, is out of training entirely, is middle-aged, has grizzled hair which he has had cut within the last few days, and which he anoints with lime-cream. These are the more patent facts which are to be deduced from his hat. Also, by the way, that it is extremely improbable that he has gas laid on in his house. (Doyle 2012, 921–923)

Of course, Watson is perplexed, and most readers may be also. How does Holmes know so much about a person he has never met? Holmes explains with a series of arguments. We can read his explanations and fit them into an argument form. For example, the argument for the man being an intellectual:

The hat is large.
Only men with large heads buy large hats.
Large heads must have large brains.
A large brain means a person is smart.
Therefore, the hat's owner must be highly intellectual. (paraphrase
of Salmon 1963, 3)

Challenge students to evaluate the argument using the questions we asked in this chapter. Do the statements add up? (Yes.) Are the statements true? (No.)

Ask students to read with the purpose of finding the arguments that Holmes uses for all of his conclusions (for example, the statements that lead to "he has a sedentary life"). Use the graphic organizer shown in Figure 4.4 to help students see how the statements lead to the conclusion. When they have completed the organizer, ask students to evaluate the argument. Do the statements really lead us to the conclusion? Is each statement correct?

FIGURE 4.4
Graphic Organizer for Building Arguments

Directions: Using the deductive methods of Sherlock Holmes, list statements that will lead to a logical conclusion such as "the man is highly intellectual."

APPLICATION IN SOCIAL STUDIES

Several news channels are available on cable networks. They cover the events of the day, and often follow the report of a story with reflections from commentators. We are aware that different channels have different biases, but our students likely are not so savvy about media. To help them gain perspective, ask them to watch a commentary from Fox News and a commentary from MSNBC about the same topic. As I write this, the Supreme Court has just made a decision about the Affordable Care Act. One network insists that the decision was horrible, whereas the other praises it. Which statements led to those conclusions? Did the statements add up? Does each statement strike you as true? (Remember, we are thinking of first impression here and will demand proof in the next chapter.)

ARGUMENT IN PROGRESS

In thinking about the argument at the end of the previous chapter, I realize that it passed the second and third tests: the premises led to the conclusion and the premises were true. But I hadn't considered that there might be other ways to support the idea that big tests are bad. After thinking further, I decided to create new premises. Yes, many people can identify with the amount of instructional time lost to test prep, but *all* people can relate to the amount of money diverted to standardized testing. I chose the latter point as a different path to the same conclusion:

Schools are strapped for cash.
Testing costs schools millions of dollars.
High-stakes testing is bad.

The first two statements support the conclusion, and I believe that both statements are true.

CHAPTER 5

Prove It!

W e're making progress! We are working through the process of creating good thinking: understanding the building block of arguments, thinking of multiple ways to get to a conclusion, and checking to see whether our statements add up and are true. Now we'll focus on the last steps. What if there is no agreement about some of the statements in our argument? How do we prove the truth of those statements? We use evidence: finding support for each statement, making sure the evidence is relevant, and verifying the sources.

A cautionary tale: When I assigned a research project to my students, I gave them a project organizer. It included turn-in dates. For example, fifty note cards by April 28, an outline for the paper by May 6, a rough draft of the paper by May 14, the final paper by May 28. In retrospect, Step One was an absurd request. Get fifty note cards? What should be on them? I never offered one lesson about that. I had lessons about how to take notes (as opposed to copying whole passages) and lessons about where to look for information, but I never taught a lesson about what information *is*. How do students know what constitutes good information? They don't. Just because *information* is a common word does not mean students understand what we mean when we ask them for information, and inevitably they would turn in very odd bits of trivia on those note cards.

Likewise, *evidence* is a common word, so we feel comfortable saying, "Find evidence for your statements." While doing research for this book, I was unable to find one teacher who specifically taught students the definition of *evidence* and had lessons showing various types of evidence. Students looking for a statistic, a quote from an expert, or a valuable example take an approach to research that is different from the one taken by students who are looking for "evidence." They have more focus and a clearer goal in mind. A little instruction about such a crucial word before we set students on the task will increase their likelihood of success.

In the world of formal logic, a statement without evidence, without support, is called an assertion. For advanced students, we may introduce that word and explain how to use it to dismiss an opponent's statements: "How has the other side responded? Why, with mere assertions! Worthless statements!" For every student, we need to stress that each statement must be supported and able to withstand a challenge. Remember those playground disputes we had as children? At some point, we'd say, "Oh yeah? Who says?" We need to bring that thinking into our classrooms. Yes, we need to make sure the challenges are in a more polite tone of voice than the one we used on the playground. But we also need to create a habit of asking for proof every time students make a statement.

Think back to the examples in Chapter 4, which were generally safe arguments.

We have valuable things.
Locks protect valuable things.
We should have locks.

We aren't likely to hear the rejoinders "Oh yeah? Who says?" when we make safe statements such as "Locks protect valuable things." Yet very few arguments are built with universally accepted statements, so we should prepare for pushback. What about this example from Chapter 4?

Ice caps are needed to moderate temperatures on Earth.
Carbon dioxide emissions are causing ice caps to melt.
Most of the carbon dioxide emissions are from human activities.
We have to pass laws to limit the human activities that emit carbon dioxide.

Would you ask me to defend some of those statements? I hope so. Often, I fear, students do not have the immediate skeptical reaction we have. They tend to accept statements at face value without critically evaluating them. Undoubtedly you have experienced this in your classroom. A student bounces in and exclaims, "I saw a video about food additives, and we have to stop adding chemicals." Such a statement should be followed by comments from listeners: "I wonder if everyone agrees" and "We should do a little research to see if all of the statements in the video are true." But that's unlikely to happen unless we teach students to expect, demand, and demonstrate proof.

START A CHALLENGING HABIT

Jess is a fifth-grade teacher in the Chicago area. When she prepares for literature discussion groups, she has her students spend time thinking of ways to respectfully challenge the arguments their peers will make. Jess creates the mind-set that no statement should be accepted without question. Every student knows they will have to support every statement. The class comes up with specific questions to ask, and the questions are posted on an anchor chart:

> *What is your evidence for that?*
> *How does that prove what you are saying?*
> *Is there something in the text that backs up that point?*
> *Is that good evidence?*
> *What about the other evidence?*
> *So?*

"It is then amazing to hear the kids using those questions respectfully and to hear other students support their arguments with evidence," Jess reports.

I like the inclusion of the word *respectfully*. As I said, we think of a certain tone of voice as we read "So?" or "So what?" but we have to realize that these are important, needed questions once the pejorative inflection is removed.

Jess extends the lesson by having students notice evidence in writing. Students analyze many mentor texts to look for the ways in which writers support their arguments. She points out where authors have backed up their arguments with specific examples, analogies, statistics, and so on. Students begin to see how evidence is used and realize that some ways of supporting arguments are better than others, as we'll see. They learn to demand proof for every statement, back up their claims, and search for evidence in texts.

WHAT IS EVIDENCE?

Of course, as I mentioned earlier, telling a young child to identify "evidence used to support . . . claims" or to "focus on evidence-based writing," using the language of the standards, has little value if the child has never learned what evidence is or how to use it. One teacher I interviewed for this book reported that she had students use different-colored markers for "evidence, facts, etc." Wait. Aren't facts a type of evidence? And "etc."? Isn't that really a way of saying "I don't know what else"?

Let's firm up our own understanding and be very specific about language. Teach students these five types of evidence:

- Facts

- Numbers

- Quotes

- Examples

- Analogies

Let's take a look at each of these.

Facts

"As a matter of fact . . ." "In fact, most . . ." "The fact of the matter is that . . ." These are common phrases that suggest universal acceptance. When speakers use these phrases, we expect to hear something true.

Actual, verifiable, indisputable—these are qualities of facts. We can think of many statements that are factual:

All men are mortal.
Humans need water to survive.
Gravity will cause the anvil to fall on Wile E. Coyote's head.
Electrons have a negative charge.
The sun rises in the east.
Hurricanes rotate in a counterclockwise direction.

We can also think of many arguments that can be supported with facts that achieve the level of certainty that the word *fact* implies. Here are some examples:

Statement (Fact): The outside of the balloons pick up electrons from a wool scarf.
Statement (Fact): Electrons have a negative charge.
Statement (Fact): Like charges repel.
Conclusion: When we rub the balloons with a wool scarf, the balloons will repel.

No one would challenge any of these statements. There is universal agreement in the scientific community that electrons are negative and like charges repel. Unfortunately, most arguments are not built with such airtight premises. Consider these "facts":

The sun goes around the Earth.
Girls are not as good at math as boys.

These were widely accepted facts at one point but are perhaps less accepted now. Stress the fact that "facts" have a range of reliability: what we "know" at one point may be subsequently proven false.

Colleen is a teacher in New York. She teaches her fifth graders about the Westward Expansion of the United States. She shares many facts with them: the dates that Lewis and Clark explored new territories, the date of the Louisiana Purchase, the requirements of the Homestead Act, and so on. Then, she reports, "We also discussed how we could gather facts from primary source pictures as well." From photos taken during the time period, students come up with facts such as these:

Settlers went west in covered wagons.

Water was carried in barrels.

Often, a man with a gun rode next to the driver. [Yes, this is the origin of the phrase my children used often in the battle to get to ride in the front seat: "I call shotgun!"]

Horses were used for transportation and pulling.

Many travelers walked.

As students write about what it was like to settle the West, all these facts will be used as evidence.

Numbers

Numbers include statistics, surveys, or any type of measurement. For simplicity and to avoid ambiguity, tell students that, if a number is present, the information will fall into this category. Some numbers seem solid:

There are fifty states.

In cases such as this, students will say, "That's a *fact*, right? It's totally true!" No, it's a *number*. In the interest of simplicity, no matter how certain a number seems, we must insist that students avoid labeling numeric evidence as facts. (By the way, there are forty-six states. Four members of the United States are "commonwealths.")

Many pieces of evidence fall into this category, including graphs or charts.

The average salesperson made $1,000 last month.

Eighty percent of students on Team 8-1 say they are tired every school day.

Eliminating funding for this program will save the federal government $40 billion over the next ten years.

We like numbers and feel reassured when things can be quantified. We need to teach students that numbers really fall on a sliding scale of truth. That an oxygen atom has eight protons is certain; that 98 percent of North Korean voters chose Kim Jong Il is less certain. Numbers can be misleading. Teach students some ways we can be deceived.

Imagine being asked to join in a pyramid sales program. The promoter makes the first claim about the $1,000 sales commission. After investigation, however, you discover that one person made $10,000 but the other nine people on the team made nothing. That's an average of $1,000 all right, but 90 percent of the people get no money for their efforts. Consider the Team 8-1 statistic. Would it be important to note that, of the 126 students on Team 8-1, only 10 were asked about being tired? Let students know that it is important to see how the numbers were created.

Finally, let's think about the savings from cutting a federal program. Forty billion seems like a large number, but when that amount of money is spread over ten years, we'll save only $4 billion a year, which is minimal in a federal budget of more than $4 *trillion* a year. We could more accurately claim a savings of "one-tenth of 1 percent," but somehow that version seems less impressive. (I talk about why we might choose to say "forty billion" instead of "one-tenth of 1 percent" in the next chapter.) Let students know that the context of the numbers matters.

We struggle with numbers as we grade, don't we? What do we put on the report card for the student who has scores of 56 percent, 58 percent, 63 percent, 98 percent, 99 percent, and 98 percent? Is the average important, a number that she never actually received on an assignment? Is the most recent number the only important one? How far back should we go in deciding what to include in the average?

Numbers are not always as solid as they seem. Understanding that, and learning to approach numbers used as evidence with healthy skepticism, will help students as they research. Suggest that students find multiple numbers to support a statement, so they will not try to build arguments on shaky foundations.

Quotes

This is the type of evidence teachers seem most comfortable with. A quote, of course, is an exact repetition of words. We tell students to "find evidence in the text," and by that we mean "find the exact words; they are right there." For example, we have students look for lines in a literary text to support a conclusion.

> *On page 147 of the novel, the character says, "[exact words]," which proves he is opposed to burning the books.*
>
> *Look at lines forty-seven and fifty-four of the poem and you will see that the author is against the war. She says, "[exact words]."*

Erika, my teammate extraordinaire, is an eighth-grade language arts teacher, and she demonstrates finding textual quotes with eighth graders in her language arts classes. "In a lesson about poetry, we read 'Sonnet 18' by Shakespeare," she says. "The students are told that the poem is a sonnet, a love poem. We then look for evidence (quotes) that show that Sonnet 18 is about love."

Quotes can be used as evidence for claims or premises in many other lessons, too.

> ***In math:*** *All squares have to be rectangles because on page 112 it says, "Any quadrilateral with 90-degree angles is a rectangle."*
>
> ***In science:*** *"The pituitary gland doesn't just regulate growth, because on page 352, there is a list with five other things it does."*

In addition, quotes should be thought of in another way, not just "find the exact words in the text." Quotes can also mean "the exact words of an expert." The key word here? *Expert.* The credentials of the person being quoted must be impeccable. First, make clear to students that the expert must be speaking about his or her area of expertise. A neurosurgeon is an expert, but only if we are discussing medical issues. Second, let students know that experts can be bought. Doctors working for tobacco companies consistently disagreed with those who said cigarette smoking was harmful. An expert with no conflict of interest is what we are after.

Look at these examples:

> *According to Mehmet Oz, MD, "Secondhand smoke is related to loads of fatal or life-threatening conditions."*
> *www.sharecare.com/health/quit-smoking/how-dangerous-second-hand-smoke*
> *Law professor Erin Buzuvis calls the Constitution a "living and evolving document, one that set out broad principles of governance," and that's why the Court can tackle issues like same-sex marriage.*
> *www.masslive.com/news/index.ssf/2015/06/wneu_law_professor_agrees_with.html*

EVERYTHING IS A QUOTE?

Because we ask students for evidence and, an overwhelming amount of the time, mean "find a quote," students come to believe that evidence equals quote. This creates problems. You have probably experienced this in student reports:

> *According to the* New York Times *(blah blah blah),* . . .
> *According to www.something.com/crazystuff&%$#/othercrazystuff .html (blah blah blah),* . . .

If you ask what type of evidence is being shared in these situations, you'll likely be told, "Those are quotes! You always tell us to find a quote to prove what we say." Teaching students about other types of evidence will help. So will teaching them the difference between the words *quote* and *source*. A quote refers to a speaker's exact words. The source is where the evidence was found. Let's look at some examples of how we can explain the distinctions.

I read an article in the *New York Times Magazine* about a geopolitical struggle in the South Pacific. It seems many countries are competing for ownership of the small islands scattered throughout the region. The article contains all of the types of evidence, but students who have not had explicit lessons about sources will notice only quotes. A student will say, "The Spratly Islands have been claimed by China, the Philippines, Vietnam, and Taiwan. That's a quote from the *New York Times Magazine*." Do you see the problem? The student has found a fact (ownership of the Spratly Islands) and confused *the fact* with *the source of that fact*—the *New York Times Magazine*.

How about this one: "I found a quote from the *New York Times Magazine* that said the Spratly Islands sprawl over 160,000 square miles of the Pacific Ocean." What did the student really find? Evidence, but the number type, not the quote type.

Or, "To quote the *New York Times Magazine*, 'It's a lonely place, but we make ourselves busy.'" The student did indeed find a quote, but those are the exact words of Loresto, a man written about in the article.

And finally, "The Chinese are like a big shark picking off little minnows one by one." A student will say that's a quote from the *New York Times Magazine*. It is up to us to make clear that that is an analogy, a term I'll introduce shortly, found in the *New York Times Magazine*.

Be very clear to distinguish evidence from the source of the evidence.

Examples

Examples are based on observations. They may be personal anecdotes, items found in a text, or experimental results.

> *What is war like? My grandfather was in the South Pacific during World War II, and tells this story . . .*
>
> *We know she is bad tempered because one time in Chapter 2, she threw her dinner plate at her mom, and in Chapter 3, she punched her brother.*
>
> *When we dropped two Mentos into the two-liter bottle of Coke, foam went everywhere.*

Some examples lead us to great discoveries. When Newton observed an apple falling, that example led to an understanding of gravity. Some examples are misleading. When I first arrived at Oberlin College, a tearful girl was being consoled by her father: "This is not a good school. We'll find you a place where you belong." Did the example prove that Oberlin was a terrible place? We'll discuss the thinking error here in Chapter 7, but many, many students have loved attending Oberlin.

Sometimes when we ask students to find evidence in text, we ought to be more specific. For example, in a literature discussion, we may prompt students with, "What kind of character is Aunt Polly? Find evidence to support your statement." A better prompt would be, "Find examples to support your conclusion," because that prompt more specifically directs students in their search. They now know what kind of evidence to look for in the text. Follow that prompt with "Give me the page number where you found that example so I can verify the source."

Analogies

Analogies are comparisons. They show how items are related or are similar. Used well, they can not only support a claim but also clarify it and give it power such as the way metaphors illuminate language. Yet analogies are perhaps the trickiest form of evidence. They are valuable only if genuine, important similarities exist. Consider the following analogy used as evidence:

> *If the Keystone pipeline is built, it will be like the Alaskan pipeline. Here is what happened in Alaska . . .*

Is a pipeline built in Alaska really similar to a pipeline built in Iowa? Because of geographic and climate variations, the experiences in one region may not be the same in all regions. Are the pipelines more alike than they are different?

Or these examples:

> *The War on Drugs is just like Prohibition. Prohibition failed.*
> *Breathing exhaust fumes while stuck in a traffic jam is like breathing in secondhand smoke.*

Is banning alcohol similar to banning cocaine, heroin, and marijuana? Are all of those substances similar? Are the chemicals in exhaust the same as the chemicals in smoke? Do they both cause diseases such as cancer? If there is broad agreement that the elements in the analogy are alike, the analogy will work.

Analogies are tricky, but they are also a popular form of providing evidence for claims. How many leaders have been compared to Hitler, for instance? How many athletes have been touted as the next Michael Jordan/Derek Jeter/Serena Williams? We'll talk about why these may be useful bits of rhetoric in Chapter 6. Here, however, we want to stress the need to make legitimate comparisons. For any analogy, require students to list the ways in which the things being compared are similar. Also, require students to list the dissimilarities. A good analogy will have more similarities than dissimilarities. Caution students to look for a "fatal flaw," because sometimes one key difference will ruin the comparison. Both reactors use the same fuel? Check. Both reactors are made of the same materials? Check. Both reactors are built by the same company? Check. Everything looks good until we discover that one of the reactors sits on the San Andreas Fault.

All of Them at Once

We can support a statement with any or all of those types of evidence. Let's imagine a student trying to argue that children should not play football. He builds this argument:

No child should be put at risk for harm.
Football is a harmful sport because of concussions.
No child should play football.

He isn't worried that people will challenge the first statement. Indeed, as we discussed in Chapter 3, he may just leave it out, realizing that everyone will fill in that blank for him. He wants to find support for the second statement and tracks down evidence of every type.

Fact: Concussions can cause seizures, dizziness, vision problems, and mental impairment.

Numbers: Thirty-four percent of high school football players have had concussions.

Quote: "Neurosurgeons and other brain-injury experts emphasize that although some concussions are less serious than others, there is no such thing as a 'minor concussion.' In most cases, a single concussion should not cause permanent damage. A second concussion soon after the first one, however, does not have to be very strong for its effects to be deadly or permanently disabling." www.aans.org/patient%20information/conditions%20 and%20treatments/concussion.aspx

Example: Tyler Lewellen, age sixteen, died from a head injury while playing for a Riverside, California, high school.

Analogy: A helmet-to-helmet hit in football can be as violent as a severe car crash.

IDEAS IN ACTION: CREATE A TOPIC BANK

In every subject, students make statements that demand proof. Make a list of them and use them for demonstration purposes. We aren't going to discuss the statements at length just now. Rather, we are going to use them for teaching about evidence. These authentic topics will serve as better starting points than topics that are irrelevant to students. Here are some that I collected recently:

GENERAL SCHOOL TOPICS:
School uniforms reduce bullying.
Using smartphones in school is a good idea.
We should start school later.
Recess should be longer.

READING TEACHERS MAY COLLECT TOPICS SUCH AS THESE:
Winnie the Pooh is a very caring bear.
Brian should not eat the berries.
Atticus's main character trait is compassion.
Should the library have books with swear words in them?

Solar energy would reduce pollution.

Big money is influencing elections.

It would be good if children who were brought to the United States by parents who entered illegally got in-state tuition.

Colleges make a lot of money off of student athletes.

Pluto is not a planet.

Climate change is altering weather patterns.

Large, sugary soft drinks cause health problems.

Marijuana is less dangerous than alcohol.

All students should be vaccinated.

Geometry is the most useful area of mathematics. (Pun intended!)

Calculus is not important in later life.

Ask students to think about what type of evidence could be used to prove these statements. Of course, they will often find more than one option. Have a discussion about sufficiency of evidence. How many pieces of evidence will you need to remove all doubt about your assertion? In some cases, not many. One excellent example of something wonderful that Pooh did will prove he is a caring bear. On the other hand, proving that elections are swayed by money might need some numbers (statistics about money spent), an example of an election that was altered by big spending, and some quotes by political scientists.

Adding evidence is important. Sometimes, however, students randomly add evidence in an attempt to meet our requirements. How can we get better results? Tell students that they must complete three jobs to make sure that the evidence is effective.

Job One: Is There Evidence for Every Statement?

We want every statement to be supported. Yes, some statements are universally accepted—the sun rises in the east—but get students in the habit of backing up every statement. An easy way to accomplish this is to use an organizer such as the one shown in Figure 5.1.

FIGURE 5.1

Graphic organizers to help students find evidence for all statements.

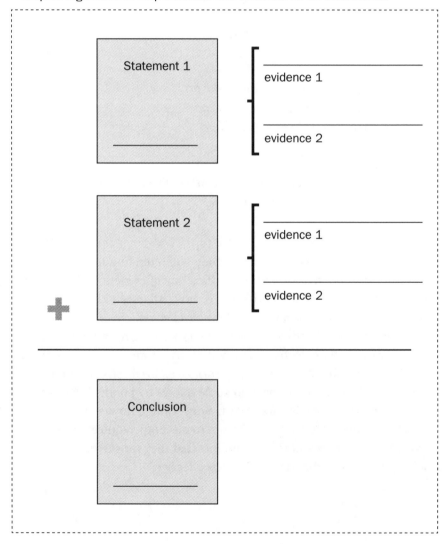

Job Two: Does the Evidence Match the Point?

When I think back again to my initial attempts to help students find evidence for their statements, I realize I failed miserably. Remember, I told students that they had to have fifty note cards by April 28. Students started putting anything and everything down on the note cards. Relevance? Who cares? We gotta have fifty note cards! I created note-taking monsters rather than researchers who thought critically. Although note cards may be anachronistic now, the problem I encountered remains a concern. When I asked for proof that concussions cause health problems in later life, I got information about

- how many concussions occur in a year,

- which sports have the most concussions,

- the NFL policy about concussions,

- how football helmets have changed,

- a parent movement to ban Pop Warner football,

- a law firm that represents people with head injuries, and

- symptoms that indicate a concussion has occurred.

The last of these examples is at least close: it discusses health issues. None of that information, however, tells me one thing about long-term effects of concussions.

Cathy, a sixth-grade English teacher in Englewood, Colorado, circumvents the problem through multiple lessons about avoiding quote dumping, "not just inserting a random quote to make the writing sound intelligent." Students discuss how to determine whether the quote backs up the point. They are told to add quotes and, importantly, given direction about *relevant* quotes.

How can we teach students to make the evidence match the point to be proved? With older students, introduce the word *relevant*. With younger students, stress probing for the connection. Look back at the questions Jess has her class ask. Highlight "How does this prove what you just said?"

Winnie the Pooh is a good friend.

(Evidence?)

Example: He rushes home to get a balloon for Eeyore.

(So? How does that prove the point?)

Friends try to make each other happy.

The Chinese lead the world in solar energy production.

(Evidence?)

Number: In the last ten years, the cost per watt of solar energy in China has gone from more than four dollars to less than a dollar.

www.bloomberg.com/bw/articles/2014-11-06/chinas-solar -power-push

(So? What does cost have to do with production? Cost going down does not prove that they produce more solar energy than anyone else.)

New Number: China produces thirty-three gigawatts, more than the twenty gigawatts produced by the United States and more than Spain, Italy, and the United Kingdom combined. Their production leads the world.

www.bloomberg.com/bw/articles/2014-11-06/chinas-solar-power-push

Job Three: Comparing Evidence

Evidence is not created equal. In each of the five types, inequality exists. Which type of evidence best supports the idea that climate change is occurring, that boys are losing interest in school, that students should have the right to pray on school grounds? Is one quote as good as another quote? Is your expert as good as my expert? In addition, between one type of evidence and the next, inequality exists. Is your one example as good as her survey? Is an expert opinion better than some statistics?

Younger students will struggle with understanding why some types of evidence fit a situation better than others, but older students need to be able to evaluate the use of evidence. That entails not only noticing whether evidence is present but being able to recognize if the evidence is high quality. "My dad says there are millions and millions of illegal immigrants" is a big step down from "According to the Census Bureau, there are twelve million undocumented immigrants."

IDEAS IN ACTION: MY FAVORITE SOURCE

Mark has an activity that he uses with his seventh graders in Washington State called My Favorite Source. "In this activity," he explains, "students examine a variety of sources on a single topic and need to decide which source is best for their purpose." He asks students to write a short paper to explain what their "favorite" source is and why. Notice that this is another way to reinforce building an argument. Students may compare two expert quotes and use an argument such as this one:

> *Professors are more qualified than TV commentators.*
> *Ms. _____ is a professor.*
> *Ms. _____'s quote is better.*

Students may be comparing two numbers, a number versus a quote, and so on.

Mark extends the activity by creating a poster that has two pieces of evidence on some topic. As students leave the room, they vote by making a mark on the poster under the piece of evidence that they think better supports the conclusion. The vote is an exit ticket, and the poster may be used as a discussion starter the next day.

IN PRACTICE

Sandy's class participates in DARE training, Drug Abuse Resistance Education. A police officer from her town comes into the classroom to educate students about the dangers of drugs. As the officer is presenting information, students take notes. At the end of the presentation, Sandy asks the students to examine the types of evidence presented during the officer's talk. She points out to students that they don't need to categorize *everything*. Some statements are, well, just statements. If we say, "Good morning, class," it is not necessary to ask, "Is that a fact? Is it a quote? What kind of evidence is it?" Students get so involved in looking for evidence that they can go overboard.

Sandy points out that, as Officer Elias shares techniques for resisting drugs (for example, walk away from the situation), students don't need to worry about categorizing each technique. If a student says, "I don't think that idea will work," we may *then* want some evidence of its usefulness (an example of when the strategy worked), but Sandy reminds students that evidence *supports* statements. She uses the form shown in Figure 5.2 and has students categorize the information in their notes.

FIGURE 5.2

Creating Categories of Evidence from Note Taking for the DARE Essay

FACTS	Self-medication = deciding on your own whether to take medication.
	Tobacco contains nicotine (a drug).
	Alcoholism means being addicted to alcohol.
	Tobacco damages the respiratory system (lungs).
	Hospitals, clinics, YMCA help people with addiction.
NUMBERS	400 harmful chemicals in marijuana.
	40 substances in tobacco that cause cancer.
	75,000 alcohol-related deaths in United States each year.
	Midnight–3:00 a.m., 77 percent of crashes are related to alcohol.
	Legally, 18+ can buy/use tobacco, and 21+ can buy/use alcohol.
QUOTES	"Heroin is the most dangerous drug, in my opinion." —Officer Elias
	"Every time I go on a call, I have to think about all of the risks involved and what could happen." —Officer Elias
	"Think about the long-term effects of your decisions, and not just ten minutes from now." —Officer Elias
EXAMPLES	Officer Elias's mom died of cocaine overdose when she was 17.
	Over time, the appearance of meth addicts looks disgusting and older (photos).
	A Brooklyn Park teenager was drunk, got dropped off, and couldn't get inside (freezing outside).
	Mom left young child in car while she drank in a bar.
ANALOGIES	Taking meth is like playing Russian roulette. One time could kill you.
	Quitting smoking is like going on a diet. Almost no dieters ever succeed.
	Driving drunk is like driving with a loaded gun. You could kill someone.

What would have been a jumble of "facts" becomes a lesson in evidence as well as a lesson about the harmful effects of drugs. Students learn to be more aware of the types of evidence without adding some special "evidence unit" of instruction.

Sandy reinforces the concept with the handout shown in Figure 5.3. In the course of everyday instruction, we run across many topics that have arguments and evidence embedded in them. The first few topics are filled in to model the thinking she expects. Students will fill in the table as the topics come up during classes.

FIGURE 5.3

Five Types of Evidence Topic Bank

*FACTS   *NUMBERS   *QUOTES   *EXAMPLES   *ANALOGIES

Statements of Conclusion	Type of Evidence	Piece of Evidence
School uniforms reduce bullying.	Example	My school has uniforms, and little bullying happened this year (compared to last year without uniforms).
	Number	Survey results that show 67 percent fewer bullying incidents based on clothing compared to last year.
Using smartphones in school is a good idea.	Analogy	Smartphone use in school is like students having a minicomputer in their hands all the time to do research and school activities.
Colleges make a lot of money off student athletes.	Example	Yale didn't have sports last year. This year, they added sports and made lots of money for their college.
	Number	Yale didn't have sports last year. This year, they added sports and made $5 million.
Pooh's main character trait is compassion.		
Solar energy would reduce pollution.		
Large, sugary soft drinks cause health problems.		
Marijuana is less dangerous than alcohol.		
Abstract art is the most widely known art style.		

IDEAS IN ACTION: REQUIRE EVIDENCE FOR "BECAUSE" STATEMENTS

When we ask students to explain their position on some issue, we often get a "because" statement. These comments came from the discussion in class:

> I disagree with the first teacher in the story because she wants everyone to do exactly what she says.
> I agree with Ore because he is himself and no one is like him.
> I agree with Abby because I am not creative. I usually want an exact answer like math, but I would like to draw my own thing.
> I agree with Gabe because I need rules because I have grown up with rules because my parents are both teachers.

When you see or hear the word *because*, a student is offering a statement that requires support. Ask your students to provide evidence to support every "because." *Because she wants everyone to do exactly what she says.* Where is the proof for that? In this case, the student can quote the text—it's right there. *Because . . . no one is like him.* Is there proof for that? Are there examples of behavior that are unique to him? Notice that one student already provided evidence: *because I am not creative* came with the supportive example *I usually want an exact answer like math.*

This reading activity becomes a listening activity, a speaking activity, and a reasoning activity.

IDEAS IN ACTION: COLLECT EVIDENCE

Build a file of statements and evidence. Some of them can come from units you already teach. Sandy used annual DARE training to get started. I invited a guest speaker from the Children's Hospital of Colorado to talk about vaccinations. Jeremy is in favor of mandatory vaccinations. He asked, "Is it right for one child to bring a preventable disease into class but another child can't bring in peanuts?" We noted that he was really offering evidence to support requiring vaccines for all. Assign students the job of looking in text, on TV, and online to find examples that demonstrate good use of evidence. Categorize them by type of evidence: statements backed by facts, statements backed by quotes, statements supported with examples. Jeremy's statement went into the analogy file; he's comparing protecting students from allergens to protecting students from communicable diseases. Over the course of the year, you will develop a large number of samples to use in modeling how to support statements. Sometimes, students will bring in examples that can be used to demonstrate irrelevant evidence (the evidence does not prove the point) or weak evidence (the author of the quote is not an expert). Use those for teaching tools, but do not add them to your file.

APPLICATION IN ART

Bill McBride uses pictures to teach argument. Yes, some paintings are just good to look at, but many paintings are attempting to make a statement. Picasso's *Guernica* is an example. That painting is widely seen as an antiwar statement. Bill asks students to identify the argument. If the conclusion is *the Spanish Civil War is horrible,* what statements does the painting suggest that would lead to that decision? Students will likely create a syllogism: death is horrible; war causes death; war is horrible. He challenges students to look for evidence in the painting that would prove those statements. Students will probably suggest that the wailing mother holding a dead child supports the first statement. Art appreciation, art history, world history, and thinking skills are all involved in his activity.

APPLICATION IN HISTORY

Look up photojournalist Lewis Hine. He had a huge effect on eliminating child labor in America. How did he do it? He took photographs of children working. Each photograph was part of an argument. The photos made strong statements about poor working conditions and the inappropriateness of using children as cogs in industrial machines. Find, or have students find, other images that have been used as arguments for historical change.

APPLICATION IN READING

Have your students read the story "The Little Boy" by Helen Buckley. In the story, a creative young boy comes into class and is asked to draw a flower. The boy starts to use every crayon in the box but is stopped by the teacher. She tells him to copy her drawing of a red flower on a green stem. The story suggests that the boy loses his ability to be creative that day.

As teachers, we typically have students read a story and then we ask, "What was the point?" or "What was the author trying to say?" or "What is the message of that story?" Let me suggest another way to phrase those questions: "What are we supposed to conclude from this story?" Yes, stories are arguments, too. Authors are trying to persuade readers to accept some point of view. Can we flesh out the argument in "The Little Boy"? How about this:

Creativity is a good thing.
Telling a child what to draw ruins creativity.
Never tell a child what to draw.

You may phrase it differently, but the author wants us to conclude that we should not interfere with youngsters' free-flowing styles.

We can examine this story the way we examine all arguments: Do the statements lead to the conclusion? Yes. Are the statements or premises true? Well, we can easily imagine a society that would disagree that creativity is good. Some societies may value order and predictability over freethinking. That point aside, challenge students to look for evidence to support the second statement. What kind of evidence was used? There are no facts, numbers, quotes, or analogies in the story. The author uses an example. When the boy goes into another class, he is unable to be creative, and based on that one example, we are supposed to think that his first teacher wrongly stifled his creativity. Extend the activity by asking students if they believe that one example is sufficient to prove the point. Should we ever accept an idea based on only one example? More about that in Chapter 7.

APPLICATION IN SCIENCE

When I taught sixth-grade science, I had a "kitchen chemistry" lab about acids and bases. I set out cupped trays from our science kit, each of which had white powders in the six little cups: baking soda, powdered sugar, talcum powder, salt, baking powder, and crushed antacid tablets. Students had two dropper bottles, one filled with water and one with vinegar. Students also had litmus paper, thin strips of paper that turns blue if the substance is a base and red if it's an acid. The challenge? Identify whether a "powder" is an acid, a base, or neutral.

Students had to look for evidence. If an acid meets a base, a chemical change occurs and gas is produced. Is that what happened when drops of vinegar touched the baking soda? Did the litmus paper change color in the salty water? Students did not all agree on the appropriate labels and had to explain why they thought their interpretations of the results should be accepted. They provided conclusions and explained how the evidence supported those conclusions. Notice again that an argument activity sneaked into normal instruction.

APPLICATION IN SOCIAL-EMOTIONAL LEARNING

"Everyone hates me!" Chandra said as she came into the counseling office.

Lindsay, the school's counselor, often hears comments similar to that from middle and high school students at her school in the Seattle area. She works students through their problems in part by teaching reasoning. Sometimes, as part of helping the student, she, too, becomes a teacher of thinking skills. Notice that Chandra's statement is a conclusion. Chandra has not told Lindsay the statements that lead to that conclusion, so Lindsay asks for elaboration. In doing so, Chandra explores evidence and how to evaluate it.

LINDSAY: What is the evidence for that?

CHANDRA: Amanda gave me a dirty look.

LINDSAY: That's one person. Does that prove that everyone hates you?

CHANDRA: Well, also, at lunch, when I went to sit with Amanda and some others, they said the table was full.

LINDSAY: Hmm. That still seems like less than "everyone," doesn't it?

CHANDRA: OK, so it isn't everyone, but my friends hate me now. I don't even want to be in this school anymore!

LINDSAY: Let me ask you a couple of questions. When did Amanda give you a dirty look?

CHANDRA: In the hallway before Period Two. I was walking past her.

LINDSAY: Did you say hi to her?

CHANDRA: No, because I was still mad about her texting her brother that I liked him and then he texted everyone!

LINDSAY: So the dirty look may not be because she hates you but because she thinks you snubbed her and she might think you hate her? Maybe that dirty look doesn't mean what you think it means.

CHANDRA: But I still didn't get to sit with her and our friends.

LINDSAY: Was the table full? Was there a seat available?

CHANDRA: No, but they coulda saved me a seat.

LINDSAY: Then who would be in my office saying they were left out? Maybe it just didn't work out for you today at lunch.

Lindsay models good thinking, and using and evaluating evidence to begin to defuse a typical adolescent problem. Some of the charge is taken out of the situation so she can get to the next steps showing how to get the friendship back on track.

ARGUMENT IN PROGRESS

At the end of the last chapter, I had a pretty good argument. I realize now that it lacked evidence for the statements. I decided to add evidence for my premises. I added an example to my first statement and some numbers to the second statement.

Schools are strapped for cash. *Because of a tight budget, my school has added fees for extracurricular activities that students used to be able to attend for free.*

Testing costs schools millions of dollars. *My district spends $75.00 per pupil per year on standardized tests. Testing 54,000 students cost more than $4 million a year.*

High-stakes testing is bad.

CHAPTER 6

From Argument to Persuasion

A ristotle is back in fashion. About 2,500 years ago, he wanted to discover the keys to persuasion. He came up with three categories, logos, ethos, and pathos. In the first of these, *logos*, you can see the root word for *logic*, and you are correct that logos appeals to logic. A clear-thinking, logical person will obviously be impressed by a well-built logical argument.

In education, when we ask for argument, we are usually looking for logos. Teachers and testing companies want a logical argument (with evidence). Chapters 3, 4, 5 have shown you how to prepare students for academic arguments. Aristotle realized that logos is not always persuasive, however. Logos may get us to the truth, but the goal of authors and speakers is to convince the audience of the truth. Logic does not always impress people. A brilliantly constructed argument with terrific factual support is certainly a good goal to shoot for, but if we want to move people to action, that may not be enough. Not all folks are clear-thinking, logical people. How do we reach them? People are often motivated by poor arguments that are somehow compelling. Why is a heart-wrenching story of one downtrodden individual likely to bring more money into a charity than showing the statistics about the many individuals the charity serves and explaining the balance sheet showing how much money is needed? Something beyond logical argument is involved. We want students to build good arguments, but we want those arguments to be convincing, too.

I used the terms *cold* and *hot* earlier. Argument is cold: it is made up of passionless statements that lead to a conclusion. Persuasion is hot: it consists of methods we use to get readers or listeners to care about the argument. I wrote in *Well Spoken* that, although I want students to build good talks, I also want them to know that performing the talk is the more important piece of oral communication. Great performers can make poorly built speeches seem impressive. Argument is similar: great use of the tools of persuasion can make poor arguments seem compelling. Strong arguments with persuasion added? You can rule the world.

That brings us back to Aristotle. He, too, realized that logos is not the only option for swaying the crowd. He suggested two other categories: *ethos* and *pathos*. Again, you recognize root words there. (As a side note, teaching good thinking gives us a chance to reinforce our teaching of root words. Share with students the connection between Aristotle's ideas about argument and the origins of the words *logic, logical, ethical, ethics, empathy, sympathy,* and *pathetic*.) Ethos is an appeal to credibility. Ethos in action: Look, I am a great guy. I have taught for many years and written several books. Clearly, you should do what I ask you to do and believe what I say. Trust me when I say that teaching good thinking skills to students is a great idea.

Pathos is an appeal to emotion. Pathos in action: Picture one student in your class. Visualize her typical day. She is bombarded by arguments trying to persuade her how to look, think, and behave. She is overwhelmed by the input from digital media, TV, and social media. She has no defense, no way to analyze and evaluate the messages attacking her. Do you want to leave her undefended? No, of course not. Teach her good thinking skills.

Logos, ethos, and pathos are part of our daily lives. Students enjoy learning these sophisticated terms and love looking for examples of their usage. It is great fun to play with Aristotle's ideas to make our academic arguments persuasive.

AUDIENCE ANALYSIS

There are several ways to build an argument for any given proposition, as we have seen. Let's look at one more example. Assume I want to persuade you to become a vegetarian. Which of these would be the best argument?

All animals have feelings just as the human animal does.
Factory farming, injections, and slaughtering are horrible and
 painful.
You should quit eating meat.

The environment should be protected.
Cattle raising uses enormous amounts of water, generates massive
 amounts of waste, and destroys rain forests in South America.
You should quit eating meat.

Fat and cholesterol are health hazards and lead to heart problems.
Beef and pork have lots of fat and cholesterol.
You should quit eating meat.

All three arguments add up. We could find evidence to establish the "truth" of each statement. So which one should I use to convince you?

The answer: It depends. Some readers are more likely to be moved by the plight of innocent animals being cruelly treated. Some readers are greatly concerned about our planet's environment. Some are worried about their health. Yes, we can be concerned about all of those issues at the same time, but usually one argument is more powerful than another to us. I need to do an analysis of the audience—in this case, you—to figure out which one to offer. I have to know what you value.

Car salespeople have always known this. They probe prospective buyers as soon as they walk through the door. Mileage-and-warranty person or horsepower-and-style person? Big spender or budget minded? Space for gear or easy to park? They tailor the sales pitch accordingly. Are you a logos person? "This car has great mileage and a great warranty. It has the highest resale value in its class. *Consumer Reports* ranked it number one in midsize sedans three years in a row." Are you an ethos person? "I want you to get into the vehicle that's best for you. I don't want to sell you something that isn't right. I know there are lots of shady car salesmen out there, and salesmen have a bad reputation. I'm not that type. Shop around. Look at competitors. Then let me know how I can help." Are you a pathos person? "You want something that everyone else has, or do you want to be distinctive? You've seen cars that made you look back and think, *Cool car, man!* Why not have one of those for yourself? A head-turner. Something special." Because persuasive essays and speeches are sales pitches, too, they must also be tailored to the audience.

Paul Solarz teaches fifth graders in the Chicago area. He uses Intel's Visual Ranking Tool with his students. The Visual Ranking Tool is one of several free "thinking tools" available at Intel's website. A teacher can make a list of items and ask each student to put them in rank order. An example at Intel's site has a teacher asking, "Which invention had the greatest impact on our lives?" and then listing "automobiles, immunizations, lightbulb," and so on. Each student puts the inventions in order from most important to least important and then compares that list with classmates'. Rationales must be given: Why did you put the computer at number one? (See www.intel.com/content/www/us/en/education/k12/thinking-tools /visual-ranking.html.)

As his students study the human body, Paul asks them to rank the importance of the major joints in the skeletal system. Students research various joints and learn about the joint's function. They use the ranking tool, and when all have finished, Paul has the students compare their individual ranking with the class average. He asks students to explain the argument they used for declaring that one joint is better than another. A child who loves soccer might point out that she couldn't play without good knees; a student who loves food might select the jaw that enables him to chew good food; a pianist might value finger joints the most. By extension, students grasp that arguments, like joints, have differing degrees of acceptance based upon the characteristics of the audience.

This is where I like to use the word *reason*. Rather than use that word as a synonym for statement or premise, I prefer to use it in a different, perhaps more common sense. *Reason* means "explanation." Recall that in Chapter 4, I changed the statements I used to support my conclusion about testing. What was the reason for that change? Alternatively, what was my explanation for that change? I did an audience analysis and determined that more folks would be motivated by money than by time. To be persuasive, then, means figuring out which argument is best for your audience. Let's look at some additional ways to make the logical points action-producing points.

COMMON PERSUASIVE TECHNIQUES

No matter which argument we select as most likely to succeed, there are certain time-honored ways to turn argument into persuasion. You will recognize all of these from television commercials for products, services, and candidates. I'll give examples using the arguments we created about locks and lockers in Chapter 3.

Fear: Present a scary situation, something horrible that we all want to avoid. You may be offending others with bad breath. This cute dog may be killed. That candidate will ruin the economy. The solutions? Buy my product! Give me money! Vote for me!

Every day, valuable things are stolen. It takes only one bad person. It takes only one student in our school with a hall pass to steal your stuff. Your stuff gone. Can you afford that? No? Then demand that students be allowed to have locks!

Bandwagon: Everyone's doing it! All the cool people are doing it! You gotta join the crowd!

Campus Middle School has locks. Prairie Middle School has locks. Thunder Ridge Middle School has locks. Every school but ours seems to have locks! It's time for us to have locks.

Testimonial: A famous person is used for endorsement. Unlike the quote from an expert, this person may not have actual expertise in the topic. In the world of advertising, having name recognition is good enough. A former quarterback speaking for a mortgage company? Sure! An actress asking you to save the rain forest? Why not!

Pro baseball player Miguel Cabrera goes to work every day. He puts on his uniform and takes the field . . . but not until he locks his locker in the clubhouse. Miguel Cabrera locks up his stuff, and we should be able to lock up our stuff.

Loaded words: Words have different connotations. Words have different effects. Illegal immigrants or undocumented workers? Environmentalist or tree-hugger? Conservative or right-winger? Are you "disagreeing with my opinion" or "bashing my ideas"? And which is more: fifteen hundred or one thousand five hundred? Saving forty billion dollars or saving one-thousandth of the budget? We can select powerful words to aid our arguments.

Ripped off. Unarmed robbery. Right under our noses, burglary and theft. Why? Foolish, shortsighted people who won't let us have locks.

Repetition: Simple to understand. Just repeat key ideas over and over. Say the number to call four times. Make sure we hear the slogan several times.

Want to protect your jacket? Lock it up! Want to defend your notebook? Lock it up! Worried about the cell phone you can't have in class? Lock it up!

Slogans: Quick, think of some clever slogan that is stuck in your head. Most of us can come up with a few. In fact, some of us have a hard time trying to forget them! Some become memes for our time: "Got milk?" and "Keep Calm and Carry On" morphed into many slogans.

Why not locks? We have things to protect. Why not locks? We have lockers. Why not locks? We have rights. Why not locks? (Yes, slogans and repetition often come together.)

Plain folks: We identify with people who are just like us. A regular family with kids the same age as mine are eating that food? Maybe *I* should buy that food for my family. A construction worker with a hard hat drives that brand of truck? *I'm* a construction worker who wears a hard hat, so maybe *I* should buy that kind of truck.

Devin is a typical sixth grader. He doesn't go to our school; he goes to Falcon Creek Middle School. He has a jacket with the logo of his favorite sports team on it. He has some textbooks and some notebooks. He has a model he made in the class makerspace. And all of those are locked up in his locker.

Transference: Ever notice the stuff that surrounds a politician making a speech? Some American flags on poles nearby, pictures of American heroes on the walls, and universally loved objects visible on the desk, right? These are all chosen by careful design. Advertisers noticed long ago that viewers transfer the good feelings from beloved things to the person or product being featured. Grandmothers reading to kids, farmers working in the fields, and smiling babies are all in the commercial for instant mashed potatoes? I *love* instant mashed potatoes now.

Students create a poster to put in the hallway. Illustrations surround the slogan "Why not locks?" (written in letters using the school colors), including pictures of happy students, school mascots, french fries, and the school trophy case.

Beautiful people: Gorgeous men and women use this product? I may be plain folk myself, but if I drink that cola or buy that car brand, I'll be surrounded by hunks and babes? If I use that shampoo, I'll *become* a beautiful person? Cool.

Ask Chantelle and Graham if you can put their pictures on the "Why not locks?" poster being made for the in-class debate about lockers.

IN PRACTICE

During one class period, Sandy Otto introduces logos, ethos, and pathos to her students through the use of print ads. She defines *logos* and shows a few magazine ads that appeal to logic, including "Smoking kills," an ad that has a list of twelve health dangers from smoking.

Sandy defines *ethos* and shows ads with trustworthy people (such as Colonel Sanders) pitching products. She defines *pathos* and shows an ad for a food bank that plays with our feelings by featuring a little girl asleep, holding a doll in her arms. The surrounding text: "She goes to bed hungry." In addition, Sandy found a video at YouTube about logos, ethos, and pathos that was appropriate for fifth graders.

In a subsequent class period, she introduces the persuasive techniques. She has taken the information and put it into a PowerPoint presentation. The last slide reveals the homework: go home and watch television! She gives the students a handout (shown in Figure 6.1) to guide their commercial viewing. Sandy tells students that one thirty-second commercial likely contains several techniques, and it is legal to use one commercial for multiple categories.

FIGURE 6.1

Logos, Ethos, and Pathos Guide to Television Viewing

FEAR	Scary situation, something we all want to avoid	
BANDWAGON	Everyone's doing it, all the cool people are doing it, join the crowd	
TESTIMONIAL	Famous person endorses item (may or may not be an expert)	
LOADED WORDS	Powerful words are selected for effect	
REPETITION	Ideas are repeated over and over	
SLOGANS	Clever and catchy words that we have a hard time forgetting	
PLAIN FOLKS	Identify with folks who are just like me/us	
TRANSFERENCE	Product surrounded by well-loved objects	
BEAUTIFUL PEOPLE	Gorgeous men and women using the product	

Students share their results over the next couple of classes, amazed at how often these persuasive tricks are used.

As a summative activity, Sandy asks her students to create a sixty-second commercial. The time limit is strict: television commercials are exactly thirty seconds or sixty seconds. When a show breaks for commercials, it doesn't break for *about* three minutes; it breaks for exactly three minutes, playing exactly timed commercials to fill the break. Sandy allows flexibility and creativity: students can invent a product or service or make a commercial for a product that already exists; students can use digital tools to present the commercial or can do it live; students can use one technique or fit in many; students can create visual aids or dress up as they wish.

When I did this activity with my students, I used to sneak the presentations into every subject: "Today's class is brought to you by H & M Rescue Services. Take it away, Haley and Maria!"

Or "In a minute, a video about cell division, but first a word from our sponsor. Andre, you're on." Of course you noticed that once again, one activity serves multiple purposes: listening standards about evaluating a speaker's message, speaking standards about incorporating multimedia in presentations, and standards about oral presentations are all addressed in a fun, engaging way.

APPLICATION IN CONSUMER STUDIES

Visit www.consumersearch.com. (It is always risky to recommend a website in a print book. Sites come and go.) Consumer Search claims to collect product reviews and analyze them to make recommendations. *We* don't need to survey all the reviews online. Theoretically, the site has already done that, and it provides composite reviews that quote other reviews. The top four or five rated products are presented. Have students select a product and read about it at the site. Bike helmets, garbage disposals, karaoke machines—the options are endless. Tell students to choose one of the top-rated items and write about their decision. For example, a student researching sunscreens will notice that many criteria are mentioned: the way they feel on the skin, the smell, water-resistance and protective properties, cost, the presence of harmful chemicals, and more. What should a good consumer do with all this information? Students must explain their evaluation process. Does protection outweigh everything else? Is low cost important? Notice that this is really argumentative writing: build an argument to defend your choice.

Now that students have made and defended their selections, ask them to write persuasive copy for an advertisement. Require them to include at least three of the appeal techniques discussed in this chapter.

IDEAS IN ACTION—SHAKESPEARE

Have you heard of the elevator pitch? In the business world, it is common to develop a very short talk to sell yourself or your idea. The thinking is that if you happen to be in an elevator with a bigwig, you'll have something to say between the time the doors close and when they reopen that will make the bigwig take notice. Use that idea and ask students to come up with a two-minute pitch presentation. Suggest possible pitch topics such as these:

- Create an additional scene that should be added to the new movie version of *Romeo and Juliet*. Sell the idea to the movie director.

- Create a product that the characters in *Romeo and Juliet* could use. Pitch the idea to investors who will help develop and sell the product.

- Explain to a director how *Romeo and Juliet* should be modified to make it more marketable to today's audiences.

Students need to understand the play and then extend their understanding by developing these talks. It is also a good way to introduce and practice persuasive speech.

IDEAS IN ACTION—WRITING

Kaitlyn Fischer is a fourth-grade teacher in New Jersey who uses the newspaper's Sunday circulars for discovering persuasive techniques. Before her students begin writing persuasive essays, they analyze real advertisements from the Sunday circular (for diet pills, snacks, toothpastes, commemorative plates, shampoos, and so on) and look for persuasive techniques the advertisers use. They search for slogans, testimonials, idealistic images (beautiful people), and bandwagon examples. In her words, "Students loved seeing real-world examples of persuasive writing!" Students also think about what audience the advertiser is trying to target. This simple activity includes audience analysis, media literacy, persuasive writing, and high interest.

RHETORICAL DEVICES

Style over substance. You've heard the phrase. It has a negative connotation. We can all think of a time when we thought we didn't get enough substance. For example, my wife and I went to an expensive restaurant that had beautiful plates, a carefully placed food item on each plate, and some decorative drizzle around the food. High marks for style. But the food? No big deal. I would have preferred less style and more substance. With students, we stress substance as well. But what if we can have style *with* substance? That's where rhetoric comes in.

In his book *The Office of Assertion*, Scott Crider points out that the word *rhetoric* has a bad reputation.

> Immediately after someone has distorted the truth . . . the journalist will comment, "We know that was just rhetoric."
> Rhetoric: this pejorative term now means any language, spoken or written, which is misleading or actually untrue. (Crider 2005, 1)

In ancient times, though, rhetoric wasn't so poorly thought of, and Crider seeks to defend rhetoric. He quotes Aristotle, who said that rhetoric is "the faculty of discovering the possible means of persuasion in reference to any subject whatever" (Crider 2005, 5). Rhetoric isn't bad; it's neutral. The effect depends on how we use it. Yes, people can use rhetoric to hide the truth, to persuade us that something is true when it isn't, or to persuade us to do wrong things. But rhetoric also is a way to make our arguments more appealing. Our students have built great arguments based on evidence, right? They added some persuasive tricks. But is there more they can do to persuade readers or listeners? Remember that our goal is to gain acceptance for our ideas, and to accomplish that, we have to enhance the presentation of those ideas. Rhetorical devices can help us attain our goal.

I think application of rhetoric is appropriate for older students, but noticing the use of rhetoric is appropriate for younger ages, as standards suggest. You may have some rhetorical terms floating around your classroom already. Let's organize them and group them for easier understanding.

USEFUL RHETORICAL DEVICES

A web search of *rhetoric* reveals many different lists of rhetorical terms. Some words appear on almost all lists, some terms appear on one list but not another, some lists are short, and some lists are long. I am not suggesting that this section is the source for all things rhetorical. Writing teachers will realize that I could add *metaphor, simile, personification, alliteration,* and more. A college professor might notice that *antiphrasis* is missing. Arguably, *repetition* could be in this section instead of the persuasive techniques we've discussed. Remember that our purpose is to make the rational argument more marketable, so I have listed only the devices that I believe are most useful to that goal.

> *Hyperbole*—grossly overstating the truth
> I heard a congressman say, "This is the darkest hour in the
>   history of our country" after the Affordable Care Act
>   passed. The darkest hour? Really? I realize that there are
>   reasons to dislike the act, but isn't that an overstatement?
>   I might have thought the Civil War was darker.
>   Overstatements are part of many conversations, aren't
>   they? I wrote *Well Spoken* because student presentations
>   were *boring me to death*! I must have told my sixth graders *at*

least a million times that *pilot* is not spelled *piolet*. Hyperbole adds interest and drama to statements. "I am disappointed in the decision" lacks the punch of "This is the worst decision in the history of mankind."

Stuff gets taken from our lockers all the time! *We gotta have locks.*

Understatement—saying much less than could be said

Interestingly, the opposite of hyperbole has dramatic effect also. "I was a bit unlucky today," said the man who discovered that hackers had wiped out his bank account, thieves had stolen his car, and a tornado had destroyed his house. The listener immediately thinks of how horrible his day was, and the jarring use of understatement emphasizes the disastrous events.

It's no big deal. A couple of cell phones, a laptop, a down jacket, and some books were taken from unlocked lockers last month. Just small stuff.

Euphemism—substituting nonoffensive words for words that may be offensive

At one point, the United States had nuclear missiles that we called *peacekeepers*. A weapon with enormous destructive power and the potential to end life as we know it could have been called *civilization-destroyers*, but that term seems less acceptable. *Jails* seem worse than *correctional facilities*; *put to sleep* is nicer than *killed*; *revenue enhancements* beat *taxes* every time.

Every once in a while, something gets permanently borrowed from an open locker. It hasn't been a big problem.

Dysphemism—substituting an offensive word for a nonoffensive word

Yes, euphemism has an opposite, too. Are we talking about snacks or about *junk food*? Do you want a cigarette or a *cancer stick*? Is the house a fixer-upper or a *death trap*?

An open invitation to theft. That's what we have without locks.

Allusion—adding a reference to something well known

Alluding to another event or person can change the
way we think of the subject being discussed. "The
president's actions remind me of Stalin's leadership"
cleverly gets the reader to associate the president with
a universally hated ruler. "Though he isn't Superman,
the president has done some amazing things" associates
the president with a superhero. Allusions can be subtle
ways of criticizing or supporting: The first speaker
never said, "I hate the president," and the second
speaker never said, "I love the president." They merely
planted seeds in our heads.

*Blackbeard and a gang of evil pirates aren't coming to our school to
steal from our lockers, but can we trust all students?*

Rhetorical questions—asking questions that are added for
effect

Do we want some children to go to bed hungry? Do we
want a nation that turns its back on young people? Do
we want to be selfish, nasty people ignoring our youth?
These questions are set up to force the right answer
to jump into the reader's head: protect our kids! Of
course, the questions could be set up differently to
lead us in a different direction. Do we want some old
people to go to bed hungry? Do we want a nation that
turns its back on the elderly? Should self-absorbed,
frivolous youths get more attention than adults? Now
the right answer seems to be different: protect our old
people! Sometimes the answer is provided: Are all food
additives bad? No. Should we go overboard and ban all
additives? Of course not!

*Do we want students' possessions to be taken? Do we want to
encourage theft? Do we want to continue to ban locks?*

Priming—leading the reader/listener to a certain train of
thought

An experiment: People never notice things. They never see all
the beauty that is right before their eyes. They don't notice
things right around them. You know what we need to do
more of? Now fill in the blank: *lo_k*. Did you think of the
letter *o*? Most people do. Priming sets up the situation so
the listener/reader is thinking your way. Remember that
Sandy's students wanted to protect their belongings. They
had lockers but needed something else. What did they
want? Fill in the blank to complete this word: *lo_k*. Did you
add the letter *c*? We could have used the letter *c* the first
time, but we were primed to think of the letter *o*.

IDEAS IN ACTION—SHAKESPEARE

In act 3, scene 2 of *Julius Caesar*, Brutus and Marc Antony speak after
Caesar's death. Even those of us with limited knowledge of Shake-
speare will recognize phrases from these speeches such as "Friends,
Romans, countrymen, lend me your ears." Caesar was murdered, of
course, but was the murder justified? Was it for the good of Rome?
Marc Antony's speech is an excellent example of rhetoric in action.
In small groups, let students look for examples of persuasive and
rhetorical techniques.

ARGUMENT IN PROGRESS

Let's use these ideas to heat up the argument we have created. We'll put
in some Aristotelian pathos, add a bit of fear, make use of repetition,
and toss in some rhetorical questions.

Schools are strapped for cash. Because of a tight budget, my school
has added fees for extracurricular activities that students used to be
able to attend for free. *That may not mean much to you, but it means a lot
to Owen. He loves basketball. He played on the sixth-grade team. He played
on the seventh-grade team and was the leading scorer. He won't play on the
eighth-grade team. His parents are struggling to pay rent and don't have
$120.00 to spare for Owen's basketball right now. What will he do now?
Hang out with kids who have nothing to do? Experiment with alcohol and
drugs? Lose interest in school? Who knows?*

Testing costs schools millions of dollars. My district spends $75.00

per pupil per year on standardized tests. *That's $4.5 million gone. That's $4.5 million not spent on new materials. That's $4.5 million not spent on improving facilities. That's $4.5 million not spent on more teachers. That's $4.5 million wasted.*

High-stakes testing is bad.

CHAPTER 7

That Seems Reasonable

I f our goal is to master state standards, we are probably already finished. Students have well-constructed arguments, good evidence, and knowledge about how to turn argument into persuasion. They are ready to respond to the formal writing and speaking assignments we'll give them in school and on the Big Test. But our goals go beyond standards. We want our students to think well every day of their lives, and we want them to be able to critique the thinking of others. That involves being able to demonstrate good thinking in less formal, everyday situations.

Consider class discussions. We don't want to stop the flow of the discussion to demand a formal argument:

> **SETH:** I think Atticus is quite a bit different in *Go Set a Watchman* than he was in *To Kill a Mockingbird*. He comes across as more racist.

> **JUANITA:** I partly agree, but partly disagree. He doesn't say blacks are incapable of voting because they are black but rather because they haven't been educated. It isn't a black thing, it's an education thing.

> **TEACHER:** Just a minute, Juanita. Before we respond to Seth, let's have Seth develop his argument. What are your premises, Seth? Give us the statements that lead you to believe that Atticus seems more racist. Then point us to the examples in the text that support that statement.

That kind of interjection would kill the discussion, wouldn't it? I don't suggest that we always demand full explanations of thinking. Still, there are teachable moments in casual situations, and we should be alert to them. Here's an example: I recently suggested to my wife that we needed to move. I had just read an article that shared a shocking statistic: 77 percent of car accidents happen within fifteen miles of home (www.progressive.com/newsroom/article/2002/may/fivemiles/). It is clear, I said, that we should move at least sixteen miles away from our current home in order to be safe! Anne saw things differently. That old joke was based on faulty reasoning, she said. She suggested that, because we weren't going to move, we should repaint the house.

During class discussions, we should be on the lookout for similar thinking errors. If you are in a classroom, I will bet you have some amusing examples of incorrect thinking. We typically comment when we hear the mistakes, but I'm not sure we always explain our comments. For example, there is a difference between these two:

Jaime, don't insult Vanessa.

and

Wait a minute. What just happened? Did you notice, class, that Jaime just said something about Vanessa instead of about the issue we were discussing? We never want to be mean to people whose opinions are different from ours. We can disagree with someone's idea, but attacking the person is never OK. Let's add this to our list of reasoning errors. You may hear this kind of comment called an ad hominem attack. That's a fancy way of saying the attack is on the man, not the idea.

I don't think we want to teach all of the thinking errors as an independent lesson. Avoid saying, "Today, students, we will have a lesson about thinking errors." The better approach is to familiarize ourselves with the mistakes and be on the lookout for them in discussions. Yes, these errors show up in formal arguments, too, but I think they are best addressed in common situations to encourage critical thinking at all times, not just for special occasions. When the mistake occurs, spend the extra minute to explain the problem and why it must be avoided.

COMMON THINKING ERRORS
As you review the following types of errors, you may notice that your class has trouble with some more than others.

The Problem: Generalizing
A common error occurs when a student takes one incident or example and declares a global truth from it.

> *"When I went downtown, I saw a homeless person. Denver is a really poor city."*
> *"Fast food isn't bad for you. I eat fast food and I'm fine."*

You probably realize that generalizing is a common error outside of classrooms as well: *"Global warming? Ha! We had a record low temperature in my town today."* The existence or nonexistence of global warming is not established by an isolated incident.

Advanced thinkers might also realize that we are talking about inductive reasoning when we make generalizations from specific examples. The apple fell to the ground, the stick fell to the ground, the leaf fell to the ground . . . *everything falls down.* At some point, we are justified in reaching the conclusion: gravity does exist. But how do we know when a generalization is warranted? When I taught electricity to sixth graders, we completed circuits with copper and with steel. Generalization: Metals are conductors of electricity. We continued experimenting. Rubber didn't complete the circuit; wood didn't complete the circuit. Generalization: Only metals conduct electricity! Nope, water and humans do, too, among other things. Warn students about jumping to conclusions.

A Solution
Reinforce your lessons about syllogisms. Take an example of a generalization and turn it into a full argument.

Some metals conduct electricity.
Some nonmetals don't conduct electricity.
Therefore only metals conduct electricity.

This syllogism fails the Does It Add Up? test. Students will begin to realize that making the move from *some* to *all* is a very tricky business.

The Problem: Moving from the General to the Specific

This error is the flip side of generalizing. Sometimes we take statements that are generally true and apply them to a particular situation.

> *"Winter is when snow falls in Aurora. That means it will probably snow on Christmas Day!"*
>
> *"Millions of men love to watch football. I'll bet Erik is a football fan."*

In truth, it seldom snows on Christmas Day at my house, and I couldn't care less about football. I am a baseball fan.

A Solution

Ask students whether they can recall having been misled when trying to apply a general statement to a specific situation. For example, many fifth-grade teachers in my district are in the habit of saying, "Wait till next year! Late work will not be accepted in sixth-grade classes in the middle school." I don't know why making students fear middle school is a good strategy, but many students have sleepless nights before sixth grade. They enter middle school and find out that in fact Mr. Palmer and others do accept late work, believing that the goal should be mastery no matter how long it takes.

Students will come up with other examples of "the exception to the rule."

The Problem: Derailing the Train of Thought

When you start following the comments posted on the newspaper blogs I share in Chapter 8, you will notice that the original argument is quickly forgotten. "We should reform Social Security" somehow digresses into "Today's music is ruining America," and "The Broncos have a good chance to win the Super Bowl" morphs into "Tom Brady is so overrated!" We saw the problem in the student discussion and in the Twitter conversation I referred to in Chapter 1. You may also notice the problem during class discussions.

> *I'm worried that someone will take my iPad from my locker.*
> *You have an iPad? Does it have retina display?*

And off we go. Soon, the pros and cons of various tech features replace the conversation about locks.

Sometimes the train of thought is derailed on purpose. Want to evade the issue? Change the topic.

> *True, I didn't do my homework. But isn't it important to be with*
> *family? Isn't playing outside a way to stay healthy? Do you want*
> *us to be unhealthy?*

Sometimes evading the issue is accomplished by simply ignoring the question. Pretend that there *is* no train of thought. I am surprised at how often students and adults get away with this. Candidates asked how to reform Social Security respond with something along the lines of "I want to make America great again, and that means taking care of our elder citizens." Moderators go on to the next question as if reforms had been explained. Students make the same mistake.

> *I believe we should ban youth football because of concussions.*
> *What percentage of kids playing football get concussions?*
> *I also think we should change the rules for adult football, because*
> *NFL players have serious problems.*

Insist that students stay on topic.

A Solution

For every discussion, clearly post the topic and keep it visible throughout the discussion. Whenever a comment veers off course, instruct listeners to point to the posted topic so that the speaker will instantly receive feedback and a chance to get back on track. If a relevant question is asked, post the question and insist on direct answers. Require students to keep flowcharts (discussed next).

The Problem: Changing the Burden of Proof

Remember that we want evidence for statements. Some students are good at misdirection. Instead of coming up with proof for *their* point, they may ask their opponents to assume the burden of proof.

> *Too much time playing video games hurts students. Can you prove that it doesn't?*

It's a clever and often a successful gambit. Students in the heat of debate often get flustered and begin to think that the pressure is on them to respond to the question. The correct response to the question is "I don't have to prove that gaming *doesn't* hurt students until you give some evidence that it does. It's your job to prove your statement."

A Solution

Bring a small barbell to school. Use it to symbolize burden of proof: who has to do the lifting here? When a student says, "Video games are harmful," hand her the barbell, signifying that she has some work to do. If another student responds with "Actually, video games help kids be better students," pass the barbell over to him.

The Problem: Attacking the Person

Using an ad hominem argument is common. Although we may not use the Latin phrase, we should teach students to separate the person from the issue. It is all too easy to resort to bickering: "Oh yeah? Well, you're a doo-doo head!" Listen to talk radio or commentators on news

channels for proof that this simplistic and irrational thinking often
lasts beyond childhood.

*Of course you think we should use cell phones in class. You're a spoiled
rich kid with a fancy cell phone. But some of us are just normal people
and don't have them. We're gonna be left out.*

As I noted, many of us fall into this trap. Recall the example of
Jaime and Vanessa mentioned earlier in the chapter. We can challenge
students to remove comments about the person from all discussions. I
also include statements such as "That's the dumbest thing I ever heard"
in the ad hominem category. Although such phrases may not seem like
personal insult, they can have the effect of demeaning the person more
than the idea. Ban such comments.

A Solution

Appoint a "public defender" for every discussion. The PD's job is to be
sensitive to any personal attack. He or she has the right to interrupt,
point out the infraction, ask for an apology, and offer the speaker a
chance to begin again.

The Problem: Confusing Cause and Correlation

When my school decided to cut time from recess to put in a DEAR
block (Drop Everything And Read), I asked my civics class to prepare
for a discussion about the merits of the idea. Some students defended
recess. They researched the value of physical activity and the value
of mental breaks. Some defended DEAR and researched the value of
reading time. One student discovered research indicating that students
who read a lot do better on reading tests than students who don't read
a lot. He thought the study proved that making kids read a lot would
improve test scores. Although that assumption seems like a reasonable
idea at first glance, it actually reveals an error of thinking. Does reading
a lot cause higher test scores? Possibly, but maybe good readers find
reading more enjoyable than struggling readers do and therefore read
more. In other words, they may not be better readers because they read

more; they read more because they are better readers. Just because two things occur simultaneously does not mean one causes the other. Once students get the idea that "happening at the same time" does not mean "one causes the other," they will realize that the best way to prepare for a test is to study, not to wear the lucky hat they wore when they got an A on the previous test.

A Solution

Teach students to look for coincidences. I found a graph online that "proves" margarine consumption is linked to divorce rates (see www.bbc.com/news/magazine-27537142). Share the website with your students. We aren't likely to believe that reducing margarine consumption will help us avoid marital problems, but other coincidences may seem reasonable. Teach students to look for other possible causes. When two things occur at the same time, always ask, "What else might explain this coincidence?"

The Problem: Falling for the Halo Effect

Some people are better looking, have smoother voices, or emit magical magnetism—they just seem exceptional. A bad idea espoused by a charismatic person seems better than a good idea suggested by someone else. Did the metaphorical halo around the person cause us to be less critical of her ideas? All classes have class leaders. You know as well as I do that statements made by these students more powerfully influence the class, and you know that sometimes they are wrong. Have you seen hands go down when a class leader answers a question and other students assume their answers are now unimportant?

The reverse is also true: we devalue the ideas of people who don't seem impressive. We've all had odd ducks in class, students who didn't fit in. Other students are tempted to ignore everything those students say, but their insights can enrich discussions. I mentioned in the section about ad hominem attacks that we have to teach students to attack the idea and not the person. Similarly, we have to evaluate ideas separate from the people espousing them.

A Solution

Reinforce one of your lessons about evidence: quotes. Recall that we often use an expert for an opinion. But how do we evaluate expertness? Clearly, expertise is limited in scope. A climate change expert likely will not also be an expert about coaching NFL linemen. Similarly, although some people seem to live under a halo, their expertise may be limited. We can't generalize that "everything Erik says is better than anything anyone else says." For each student in your class, find areas of expertise. Who is well traveled? Who excels at Minecraft? Moviemaking? Dinosaurs? Soccer? Cooking? Give everyone a "halo" for his or her special talent to emphasize that no one person is above all others.

The Problem: Stereotyping

A stereotype is a form of generalization, often negative. Are football players smarter or dumber than chess players? I'm guessing that you will have a knee-jerk response to that comparison. Our society has taught us to categorize football players as brawny but not necessarily brainy. Some stereotypes may not be offensive, but they may nevertheless unfairly paint all members of a group with the same brush. Elementary teachers—male or female? Surgeons—male or female? Again, I'm guessing that you will have a quick response. I'm also guessing that you will be clever enough to resist the first impulse because you see where I am headed with this example, and you can think of some nonstereotypical responses. Students may argue that stereotypes are based on *something*. After all, most elementary teachers *are* female. We should stress that speaking about an individual based on a characterization of an entire group always involves poor thinking. And using a broad brush to demean an entire class of people (such as "dumb blondes") is highly offensive. We can do better.

A Solution

Collect some pictures to show to students: an elderly man, a doctor, a man driving an expensive car, a woman wearing a fur coat, and so on. For each example, ask students to tell you everything they can about the person pictured.

She doesn't care about animal rights. She probably spends lots on makeup. She is married to a rich man.

He moves slowly. He needs reading glasses. He is a grandpa. He takes lots of pills.

Point out how such ideas involve stereotypes. We don't know these people, yet we had no difficulty inventing details about them. Ask students whether they have ever known someone who doesn't fit the mold. Encourage students to always begin with a blank slate.

The Problem: Prejudice

It is a natural inclination to prejudge in certain circumstances. We always bring prior opinions to the table. Some of our judgments are based on past experience. If I hear that you are a member of a Rotary Club, for example, I may make some judgments about the kind of person you are because I have known many Rotarians. Some of our judgments are based on stereotypes. We have opinions about people from the Deep South and from Hollywood before ever meeting them. Some judgments are based on our previous knowledge. I almost got hit by a car when I was crossing a street in Scotland. From a very young age, I was taught to look to the left to see whether there was oncoming traffic. No cars? Go ahead and cross! But in a country where they drive on the other side of the street, my preconceived notion can be deadly. Challenge students to accurately see what is in front of them rather than judge based on previously held beliefs.

A Solution

Repeat the picture lesson, but this time use edgier examples: a farm laborer in the field, a preacher in a flowing robe, a street person holding a sign that says "Anything helps," a car salesman, a nurse, and so on. Ask students if they have a positive or negative impression of the person shown. Few will have a hard time coming up with an opinion, even though we know nothing about the individuals. This exercise will make it clear that we make judgments easily.

The Problem: Bias

Bias is a close relation of prejudice. Consider the distinction in the following example. I made this comment to a friend: "My grandson is so amazingly cute! But of course, I'm biased." What happened there? I admitted that I see Graham through a different lens than others might. Or consider this: I grew up in Detroit during the 1960s, the heyday of the American automotive industry. That background shaped my perspective on cars as well as the city. If you show me a small car, I will probably look at it differently than a person from Italy, because big sedans roamed the streets of my youth. Similarly, if someone not from Detroit shares an article about the city's decline, I may have stronger emotions than he does. Neither of us prejudged, but we have different backgrounds.

A Solution

Ask students to think about their biases. Get personal. Get specific. At one high school in my district, students expect to get a car when they turn sixteen. At a different school in the district, one car serves several adults, and students do not assume their parents will buy them a set of wheels. We don't set this up as a right-or-wrong discussion but rather one about perspective. For example, if you ask students to describe a healthful dinner, you may get similar responses if your school demographics are homogeneous but very different ideas if your population is diverse. Ask them to look at common dinners from other countries. A website such as the following can open their eyes: www .huffingtonpost.com/2014/03/28/what-i-eat-around-the-world-in -80-diets_n_5043024.html.

The Problem: Noticing Only That Which Agrees with You

The term *confirmation bias* may be too sophisticated for younger students, but we can let them know that people tend to notice things that confirm what they already think. My son believes people can jinx things. I'm not supposed to comment if we have gotten almost all green lights on our way to the store. Comments will "jinx it." I suggest that I really don't have that kind of power, but he is quick to say, "See? I told you!" when we hit the next red light. Does he say anything when we get three green lights in a row? Nope. But I'll hear about every red light on the rest of the trip. All of us make this type of mistake sometimes. Once a reputation is established, we will tend to overlook counterexamples; once we have taken a position on an issue, we will see only the evidence that supports our side.

A Solution

For homework, ask students to watch some commercials on television. Prepare them in this way:

Commercials use beautiful people. Remember that transference is about surrounding a product with positive things. [Recall Chapter 6.] *For example, when we see beautiful people eating at some restaurant, we get a good feeling about that restaurant; when we see beautiful people drinking some beverage, our opinion of that beverage improves. As you watch commercials, notice all the beautiful people being used to sell various products. You'll see that beautiful people are advertisers' best transference gimmick.*

The next day, have a discussion:

What did you notice? What percent of commercials do you think had beautiful people in them? [Expect a high percentage.] *Okay, tonight, watch commercials and count the number of plain folks.*

In the subsequent discussion, it will be obvious that the number of beautiful people was too high. Students left the first class believing that beautiful people were everywhere, and what they saw confirmed that opinion. They underestimated the number of plain folks. That's confirmation bias at work. Caution students to avoid this mistake. Ask them to be on the lookout for evidence that challenges their beliefs.

The Problem: Either/Or Thinking

In one of my favorite books, *The Princess Bride*, there is a scene in which Vizzini has a battle of wits with the man in black. The setup? Two wineglasses, a packet of deadly iocane powder, and the command to choose one of the glasses to drink from. Vizzini sets out to determine which glass contains poison inserted by the man in black. He believes he will be able to use his brilliant mental calculations to choose the untainted glass. Vizzini makes up his mind and chooses his glass, and both men have a drink from their respective glasses. The man in black says, "You chose wrong." Vizzini laughs. "You only *think* I guessed wrong!" he says, revealing that he switched the glasses when the man in black wasn't looking, giving *the man in black* the poisoned one! And then Vizzini dies. What happened? Vizzini fell victim to the either/or fallacy. The poison was in both glasses. The man in black had built up immunity to the poison, but Vizzini failed to consider that option.

I actually demonstrated the problem when I discussed DEAR reading in the cause-and-correlation section earlier in this chapter. I set up the issue as "*either* reading a lot causes students to be good readers *or* being a good reader causes students to read a lot." Couldn't both possibilities be true?

A Solution

Place students in groups of three or four and offer a problem for consideration: Increasing activity might be a good way to offset childhood obesity. Should we lengthen recess in school? After they discuss this for a bit, challenge your students to move beyond either/or thinking: Is expanding recess the only way to increase activity? Can they come up with more options? Adding more movement inside the classroom? What about having longer P.E. classes or using stand-up desks? Challenge advanced students to find either/or thinking in the real world. Build the Alaskan pipeline or not? Ban pit bulls as pets or not? Many debates use either/or questions. Get students in the habit of thinking beyond yes/no or this/that.

The Problem: Misusing Facts and Figures

I mentioned in Chapter 6 that we tend to value numbers more than other types of evidence. If we can get an exact measurement of some sort, that is solid and irrefutable, right? Yes, I have a quote from the math teacher that the student is struggling in math, but to many people, that is less important than knowing that the student scored 189 on the Levels Test. I'm not going to offer an elaborate explanation of the value of data; that discussion belongs in a different book. Just let students know that numbers can be misused and "true" numbers can mislead.

I often see graphs being misused. Consider one example: Scale can be deceptive. In 1929, the stock market crashed, leading to the Great Depression. The market fell 150 points. As I write this, the stock market is down 270 points. I'll make a graph comparing the 1929 crash and today's crash, and it will be obvious that we are heading into a depression, because today's decline is almost twice as big as 1929's. That graph would be misleading, however. A different graph might show that in 1929 the market went from its all-time high of 380 to 230, whereas today's move went from 16,700 to 16,430. For another example, selections can be deceptive. Someone denying climate change will make a graph of all the days that set record-low temperatures last year. A person trying to prove that climate change is real will make a graph showing all the record highs.

In some cases, the number may be indisputable, yet we give an unwarranted meaning to it. For example, California has six times as many representatives as Colorado does. I could argue that the House of Representatives favors California, but in actuality the number of representatives is based on population, not preference. Or, consider another example: If the school carnival made less money this year, we could argue that we should change the way we run it next year. Perhaps, but there may be other reasons besides organizational strategy that could explain the decline in revenue. Warn students about using facts and figures correctly, and caution them to be on the lookout for the many misuses they will see in everyday life.

A Solution

Ask any student who introduces facts and figures to explain two ways in which the information might be misleading.

I found this survey that says 82 percent believe _____.
I don't know how many people they interviewed or if they

interviewed only one type of person, but if it's true, the survey
means _____.

This graph shows that _____. It is from a few years
ago, and it doesn't show information from outside of Colorado,
but the graph seems to prove that _____.

The Problem: Availability Bias

When you turned on your computer to check your e-mail, the top of
the page showed a headline about a shark attack and a link to a video
showing the victim. The likely result? You'll fear going to the beach,
even if the beach near your home is far from the place of the attack.
This is an example of the availability bias: the information that is most
available dominates our thinking. In this case, the most recent thing
you saw keeps you from realizing that millions and millions of people
swim in the ocean, and the chances of getting attacked by a shark are
ridiculously small.

Sometimes drama clouds our thinking. We may have recently read
or watched a news story about a child being abducted by strangers.
Is kidnapping a danger to our children? Of course we should take
precautions, but the likelihood of our child being abducted is quite
small. The recent events may have caused us to grossly overestimate
the probability that kidnappings will happen to our kids or someone
we know.

Students are very susceptible to this kind of error. They are highly
impressionable. Unfortunately, so are adults, as people in the propa-
ganda business are well aware. We will mentally latch on to what we
are exposed to even when we are exposed to falsehoods. Think of
how many of us believed that Iraq had weapons of mass destruction.
Because of the confirmation bias, we may ignore evidence that proves
otherwise. The available falsehood becomes stuck in the brain, and it
is very difficult to dislodge the misinformation.

A Solution

Reinforce your evidence lessons. Shark attacks are a serious problem? What is the evidence that supports that? Does one shark attack

yesterday in Australia support the statement "Shark attacks mean we should stay out of the ocean"? Always ask students to look for the bigger picture rather than the first impression. In addition, share information about lies that became "truths" because of frequent messages. As appropriate for the age of your students, share widely believed statements such as these:

Sugar makes children hyper.
Girls are not good at math.
Boys are not good at reading.
Touching toads gives you warts.
You use only 10 percent of your brain.
Death panels in the Affordable Care Act will decide who gets treated.
Ulcers are caused by stress.

The Problem: Saying the Same Thing but with Different Words (Tautology)

If we have done our job well, students know that they need to elaborate when they speak or write. They know that "We should turn off the lights" will make teachers ask, "Why do you think so?" As a result, students may be in the habit of adding *because* with a few additional words. Students will say something simplistic, such as "We should turn off the lights because electricity costs money." This explanation becomes a rule in their mind: say something and add *because blah blah blah,* and the teacher will be happy. Sometimes that rule holds and the phrase that follows *because* provides an explanation. Unfortunately, there are times when the phrase has no value. Here is an example:

It's good for you because it's healthy.

Notice that in that statement, I said the same thing twice. A definition of the word *healthy* is "good for you," so I could rewrite the sentence as "It's good for you because it's good for you." For older students, you could discuss the word *tautology,* which describes the practice of making a redundant point using different words. (For extension activities, encourage students to research the applications of tautology in ancient Greece, modern mathematics, and logic.)

Students often make this mistake. They believe they have provided an explanation, so we need to help them realize that they have merely repeated themselves. We have to lead them to the deeper thinking we want from them.

> *Giving everyone a laptop is expensive because it will cost a lot of money.*
> *The Second Amendment is unnecessary because we don't need it anymore.*

These statements seem sort of reasonable, don't they? They are true statements, but they explain nothing. That a laptop is expensive because it is expensive is a silly thing to say. That a laptop is expensive because it costs a lot of money seems better but is just as silly. We want students to think of the structure of arguments and provide the statements leading to the conclusion rather than state a piece of an argument in two different ways. If we conclude that the Second Amendment is unnecessary (or, if you prefer, the Second Amendment is not needed anymore), what statements would lead us to think that?

A Solution

Put students in pairs. Collect some examples of tautologies and distribute them to the teams. Challenge students to invent a *because* clause that might provide a meaningful conclusion:

> *It's good for you because it contains lots of vitamins and minerals.*
> *The Second Amendment is unnecessary because we have a strong military and don't need a citizen army.*

IN PRACTICE—USING TODAYSMEET

Sandy Otto often has discussions based on thought-provoking stories. You'll recall that, in Chapter 3, her students were discussing a story about a child who helped a butterfly escape its cocoon. In Chapter 5, they were talking about the story of a teacher who told a creative child to follow the rules. To increase participation in these discussions, Sandy splits the class into groups. While one group is in the inner circle talking about the story, another group is silently participating by using TodaysMeet (https://todaysmeet.com/). At TodaysMeet, a teacher can create a back channel, a place where students can post live comments about what is happening in the class. Teachers create a "room" and give students the link to it, and then students can comment in real time. Sandy gives students tablets from the computer cart so they can respond to what they hear from the participants in the inner circle and also add comments to one another's posts on the site. Figure 7.1 shows an example from one of Sandy's classes. In this case, students were talking about "The Lottery," by Shirley Jackson. In that story, a small town has an annual lottery. Slips of paper are drawn from a black box, and the person drawing a slip with a black dot on it is killed by stoning. In the shocking and disturbing end of the story, written just after World War II, Jackson is asking us to think about the pointless violence in our societies. Students have strong reactions.

FIGURE 7.1
Students Discuss "The Lottery" on TodaysMeet

I know what Jeff if talking about – Hitler building his army secretly 1:23 PM, Thurs, Mar 26, 2015 by

Of course it is bad as to stone someone 1:23 PM, Thurs, Mar 26, 2015 by

me too Ore 1:24 PM, Thurs, Mar 26, 2015 by

I agree with Myla who related to the hunger games where they may not have enough food and they had to get rid of people 1:24 PM, Thursday, Mar 26, 2015 by

Kellen had a good connection to Nazis, which is an allusion. We need background to understand the connection. 1:13 PM Thurs, Mar 26, 2015 by Mrs. Otto

Because Sandy lets the verbal discussion proceed without teacher input, she is free to monitor the back channel. Notice that she reinforces her lesson on rhetorical techniques with her comment about allusion.

A great feature of TodaysMeet is that the online conversation is archived and the transcript can be downloaded. Sandy uses these transcripts to look for opportunities to correct poor thinking. Just as she may take a minute to share someone's writing with the document camera, she may project a piece of the transcript.

In another instance, Sandy discovered a comment on TodaysMeet, which is shown in Figure 7.2. By monitoring the online discussion, she was able to see that some students were having trouble staying on track. She spent a little class time the following day reinforcing better discussion habits.

FIGURE 7.2
Teachers Can Use TodaysMeet to Monitor Students' Thinking

I think the author got the idea since WWII just happend. 1:26 PM, Thurs, Mar 26, 2015 by

Was she in a pit? 1:27 PM, Thursday, March 26, 2015 by

I agree with Kaisa. Maybe rocks are good, I have a pet rock named Rock. He's cool . . . . 1:27 PM, Thurs, Mar 26, 2015 by

In discussing "Harrison Bergeron" by Kurt Vonnegut, students were thinking about whether it was a good idea to give some people "handicaps" in order to make everyone "equal." For example, a beautiful person was required to wear a mask to hide her beauty. The snippet of conversation shown in Figure 7.3 may lead to a quick explanation of the error of saying the same thing twice. Sandy deleted the child's name before sharing the sample conversation and explaining that saying "everything is everything" is an example of a tautology.

FIGURE 7.3
Using TodaysMeet, Teachers Can Monitor Students' Thinking Errors

I agree with Abby B because they are making them equal. How would it make progress 2:58 PM, Thurs, Mar 19, 2015 by

I agree with Jeff because everything would be the same everything! 2:59 PM, Thurs, Mar 19, 2015 by

In addition to using TodaysMeet, Sandy encourages her students to write on a blog and to respond to one another's blogs. She uses those blogs to root out thinking errors. During the course of the year, Sandy says she usually has a chance to address most thinking errors.

IDEAS IN ACTION—COLLECT NEWS STORIES

I read a newspaper article suggesting that married people are happier than unmarried people. Many people who read the headline probably thought, *Wow, if you get married, you will become happy*. But is that true? Articles such as this are springboards to teaching reasoning. Challenge the students to spot the problem—in this case, a cause-and-correlation one. Does getting married *cause* us to be happier people? Isn't it as likely or even more likely that happier people are more likely to get married? Who wants to marry a snarly, grouchy malcontent? In other words, maybe married people are happy *before* they get married and they remain so.

This item came across my education news feed as I was writing this section: middle school students who have a strong relationship with their grandparents have fewer behavioral and emotional problems than other students. There is a strong suggestion that the relationship between grandparents and grandchildren causes good things to happen for students. Does this represent good thinking? What are other considerations? Ask students to discuss cause and correlation in relation to this news item.

Instruct students to always be on the lookout for stories that suggest causation. They are common. The provider of my e-mail account shares several stories a day on the page that I use to log in to my account. "Watching TV before bed linked to sleep disorders!" "Seniors who eat broccoli live longer!" Discuss with students whether such examples involve coincidence, whether there may be other explanations, or whether one thing really does cause the other. Sandy uses a fun article about athletes' superstitions (see www.mensfitness.com/life /sports/10-most-superstitious-athletes) to show how illogical thinking can be misinterpreted as truth. Is it likely that old shorts cause great athletic performances? What else might explain why a lucky pair of pants or a shirt inspires athletic feats?

APPLICATION IN DISCUSSIONS

It is common for teachers to assign roles when students break into teams. One person is the recorder, one the timekeeper, one the materials getter, and so on. Bring the same thinking to discussions. Earlier, I suggested assigning someone the job of public defender. Assign other roles as needed: the engineer, to keep things on track; the math checker, to challenge graphs and numbers; the bias minder, to sniff out prejudice, bias, and stereotypes; and so on. Be creative with names. Know that in creating these roles, you are also developing listening skills. Instead of a general "pay attention" request, students begin to see that there are facets to listening and that listening for a specific purpose is important.

APPLICATION IN WRITING

My students did a lot of ten-minute writings. I'd post a prompt and let them respond without interruption for ten minutes. Some of the prompts called for opinions: should we ban french fries from the school cafeteria? In a spur-of-the-moment piece, we aren't building great arguments with evidence, so student papers often reveal thinking errors. Using actual student work is much more powerful than inventing samples. With names removed, use a document camera or some other tool to share good and bad reasoning and let the class discuss it.

> *No! I love french fries. I don't eat them every day like some kids do. They are pretty expensive and I don't have that much lunch money. But even if I did, I like other things, too. Should we ban ice cream? Sometimes they serve that and it's bad for you. No kid ever died from french fries. My dad has been eating fries his whole life and he's fine. America is all about freedom. Kids should have the freedom to choose anything they want.*

Did you find some logic errors in there? Use them as discussion starters.

IDEAS IN ACTION—CREATE FLOWCHARTS

When I joined the debate team in high school, I was introduced to flowcharts. You don't get far in debate without realizing that every statement your opponent makes must be addressed to avoid comments such as "We'll assume they agree with us since they never responded to . . ." The solution was to keep a flowchart, a he-said, she-said record of every statement in the debate. I'd divide a piece of paper into four columns. When the affirmative team said, "Checking all citizens' e-mails will root out criminals and terrorists," I'd write it down in a column on the left side of my paper. In the column, next to it, I'd write my response. The third column was for their response to my comment; the fourth was for my rebuttal to that. When the affirmative team said, "Checking e-mails is legal," I'd write that under their first statement and make sure I followed that point across the page.

At the end of the debate, we could follow every thread of the debate, every statement and response. In my debate tournaments, I used four columns, as shown in Figure 7.4.

FIGURE 7.4
Keeping Track of Arguments During a Debate

FIRST AFFIRMATIVE	FIRST NEGATIVE	SECOND AFFIRMATIVE	SECOND NEGATIVE
Reading e-mails finds terrorists.	There are no documented examples of finding terrorists with e-mails.	Officials cannot reveal how many have been caught, but some have.	You gave an excuse for having no examples, but you gave no examples.
Reading e-mails is legal.	The Fourth Amendment prohibits searching e-mails.	The Supreme Court has ruled in favor of searching e-mails if the person is suspicious.	But not all of us are suspicious, so it is not OK to search all e-mails.

I don't think we need a complex spreadsheet to follow school discussions, but some sort of note-taking strategy can help students track the thinking process when reading and listening. In Chapter 1, I shared a blog conversation in which I asked a Common Core critic to provide a specific example of some bad standard. I might make a flowchart such as Figure 7.5 to keep track of the conversation.

FIGURE 7.5

Flowchart to Keep Track of Arguments During a Debate

ME	OTHER PERSON
What standard is bad?	➡ (not answered)
I'm not defending them.	⬅ Why are you defending the standards?
Which standard is bad?	➡ (not answered)
	⬅ We will have to agree to disagree.

Figure 7.6 shows how the conversational chart can be tweaked for when we are following a discussion. If a class is considering whether all children should take P.E., for example, we can enter comments for each side and keep track of responses.

FIGURE 7.6

A Flowchart to Keep Track of Arguments During a Class Discussion

PRO	CON
Obesity is a problem. Activity reduces obesity.	Overeating is the real problem, not lack of activity.
P.E. teaches teamwork and cooperation.	No, P.E. is about competition, and some kids hate it and feel like losers.
	We don't want to get sweaty and then come to class.
The P.E. teacher, Mr. Jackson, is cool.	
Boys have to run around.	That's sexist; girls like to run around too.

When a flowchart is used, it becomes easy to see whether every point is addressed, and it becomes obvious if someone gets off track.

ARGUMENT IN PROGRESS

Looking back at my argument in Chapter 5, I now see a reasoning error. To support my first premise, I used the example of my school. I was a victim of the Specific-to-the-General error of reasoning. Can I be sure that all schools nationwide are strapped for cash because *my* school started charging for extracurricular activities? I need to make sure my school is representative of many schools. The new argument:

Schools are strapped for cash. Because of a tight budget, my school has added fees for extracurricular activities that students used to be able to attend for free. That may not mean much to you, but it means a lot to Owen. He loves basketball. He played on the sixth-grade team. He played on the seventh-grade team and was the leading scorer. He won't play on the eighth-grade team. His parents are struggling to pay rent and don't have $120.00 to spare for Owen's basketball right now. What will he do now? Hang out with kids who have nothing to do? Experiment with alcohol and drugs? Lose interest in school? Who knows?

Testing costs schools millions of dollars. My district spends $75.00 per pupil per year on standardized tests. That's $4.5 million gone. That's $4.5 million not spent on new materials. That's $4.5 million not spent on improving facilities. That's $4.5 million not spent on more teachers. That's $4.5 million wasted. *And my school is not alone. Do a web search of "cash-strapped schools," and you'll see that cities and states across America are hurting, including Chicago, Kansas City, Memphis, Michigan, Arizona, and Missouri.*

High-stakes testing is bad.

CHAPTER 8

Activities to Develop Reasoning

I n Chapter 1, I pointed out that argument is everywhere and mentioned that you probably have many opportunities for teaching thinking skills. Using the information in Chapters 3 through 7, you can now be more purposeful with those activities. But what if you are looking for new ideas? As I was surveying teachers before writing this book, several sent me ideas that they have used successfully in class. Let me share some with you. Most of these approaches would be appropriate for multiple grade levels and subjects and could be turned into either speaking or writing assignments. At the end of each activity, I mention a connection with the book that I think is relevant, but it is merely a suggestion. Play with the activities. Tweak them. Do what you do to tailor instruction for your classes.

FOLLOW A NEWS BLOG

Your local newspaper likely has a blog that directly relates to one of your units of study. *The Denver Post* has forums about politics, weather, religion, sports, education, and more, for example. Look at some of the posts in your area. As I write this, a Douglas County school voucher program has just been declared unconstitutional by the Colorado Supreme Court. What was the court's argument for rejecting the program? What argument did the blog writer make when claiming that the court made the wrong decision? Of course, readers of the blogs add comments. How well did they build to their conclusions? Caution: It doesn't take long for the comments to veer seriously off course. That may be a lesson in itself about how difficult it is to stay on topic, but for the most part what we need will be available in the original post and perhaps the first few comments.

Extend the activity by asking students to write and submit blog posts. Caution: The posts are public, so be careful to protect student privacy. Instead of writing as Erik Palmer, for example, select a nom de plume. Many sites require users to sign up to post comments. Create an account using a generic name (ConcernedStudent) and your school e-mail address. You can log in and let students post anonymously.

(Chapter 4, Chapter 7)

REFUTE AN EDITORIAL

Ask students to bring in an editorial or commentary from a print or online source. Add the requirement that students can select only editorials with which they disagree. The assignment: Build the rebuttal to the argument. Students are not trying to persuade us to believe *their* position. They are only trying to make clear what is wrong with the editorial position. Maybe the argument doesn't add up. Maybe the statements are not true. Maybe the support is weak. The student's goal is to destroy the thinking behind the editorial opinion.

(Chapter 4, Chapter 5)

PLAY WITH TRUE/FALSE QUESTIONS

Find true/false questions on tests and quizzes in your curricular area. For this activity, use only questions that are false. "No nonmetals conduct electricity." "A constitutional amendment requires approval of 51 percent of the states." "A rhombus is a rectangle." Challenge students to restate the questions so that they become true. More than recognizing the error, they must build the syllogism to support the new statement. For example,

Only quadrilaterals with four 90-degree angles are rectangles.
A rhombus has four sides, but doesn't have 90-degree angles.
Therefore, a rhombus is not a rectangle.

(Chapter 3)

ARGUE FOR JOBS

Remember how Tom Sawyer conned others into whitewashing a fence for him? Ask students to think of a chore they have to do at home—taking out the garbage, cleaning the bathroom, babysitting little sister, and so on. Give students the job of persuading others to do that work for them. As with Tom, no money is involved, so students can't say, "I'll give you a hundred dollars to clean the cat litter box for me." Or turn the task around: let students create persuasive arguments to *get* some job, rather than avoid one. Want to mow lawns or babysit in the neighborhood? Want to be in charge of the remote control? Persuade others to allow it.

(Chapter 6)

SHOP AT ONLINE STORES

Every product imaginable is available at Amazon.com and other online stores. All items have product-description sections that we can use for a fun lesson about argument. As I mentioned in Chapter 7, I am a baseball maniac. I still play in a baseball (not softball!) league for adults. I sometimes look for baseball bats to use in games. The Cold Steel Brooklyn Crusher is an amazing bat . . . according to the product description. The company makes a good argument for buying the bat. That's what product descriptions really are.

Let your students search for items to buy. Maybe they will read about the five-pound gummy bear. Maybe they will explore the acne cream of the ancient Aztecs. Whatever they are interested in will work. Ask students to notice the persuasive tricks in the descriptions. Loaded words, testimonials, transference, and more are all on display. You can do a lot with this activity:

- Ask each student to select a product and create a persuasive talk about why it should be the one item the class purchases.

- Pair students and ask them to choose a product and then write a better, more persuasive product review for the item.

- If your class can afford it, buy an item. If students chip in twenty-five cents each, they can get some food items to analyze and then eat. Let the class compare the real product to its online description.

- Pair students and ask them to write a review for the product. How many stars would they give it? Let them read some reviews to get a sense of the type of writing involved. If you have an Amazon account, post the review. Writing for a real audience is highly engaging for students.

(Chapter 6)

USE PRINT ADVERTISEMENTS

Combine media literacy and thinking skills. Collect several ads from the Sunday newspaper and magazines. Look for ads with strong images: beautiful people, beautiful surroundings, sad faces, happy faces, unusual angles, and other things that catch your eye. Ask students these questions:

- Who is the target market? (For example, men ages twenty-five to thirty-five)

- What is the ad trying to achieve? (For example, persuading you to buy that car)

- What are the hidden messages in the ad? (For example, women should be thin and well made-up; men should be thin and well dressed; if you buy a hot car, hot people will swarm around you; expensive cars are the key to happiness.)

Students will be amazed at how well advertisers construct arguments. They will also become aware of the thinking involved in the argument construction. In the ad I described in the last bullet item, you will notice several issues: stereotypes (what men and women should look like), biases (Americans love fancy cars), and cause/correlation (hot cars lead to hot people).

(Chapter 6, Chapter 7)

DISSECT POLITICAL CARTOONS

I loved using political cartoons when I taught civics. Old cartoons were a fun way to introduce history lessons; current cartoons were good discussion starters; all cartoons were useful for teaching thesis statements and argument. Find cartoons in your local paper or at sites such as www.politicalcartoons.com. Cartoons offer an implied conclusion: "Drilling in Alaska will cause problems" or "Gun regulations are needed" and so on. Ask students to identify and clearly state the conclusion. Then ask them to find details in the cartoon that provide the statements that lead to the conclusion. Here is an example:

- The polar bears are floating on the only tiny piece of ice remaining to suggest that global warming has ruined things.

- There are four ocean oil rigs in the background, meaning drilling for oil in the Arctic has caused this problem.

- The polar bear is clutching her cub, who looks worried. Polar bears will be extinct.

Have students build the complete argument.
(Chapter 3)

CREATE A CLASSROOM COMEDY CLUB

I occasionally told my students dumb jokes. I tried to excuse my behavior by telling them that state law required teachers to deliver at least one horrible, teacher-ish joke per quarter. I don't think they believed me. In truth, jokes can be used to check understanding of concepts. Use a search engine to find a site with jokes for your subject area. There are sites for technology (*There are 10 types of people: those who understand binary numbers and those who don't*); math (*What do you get if you divide the circumference of a jack-o'-lantern by its diameter? Pumpkin pi*); science (*One hydrogen atom to another: That guy stole my electron. Are you sure? I'm positive*); geography (*Where is it 90 degrees but always cold? The north and south poles*); and more.

We can dissect the reasoning in corny jokes as well. "Ninety degrees"? An improper generalization: *degree* does not always refer to temperature. "I'm positive"? A syllogism: hydrogen atoms have one proton and one electron; all electrons have a negative charge; taking away the electron leaves one positively charged proton; the atom has a positive charge.

(Chapter 3, Chapter 7)

SIMULATE A PUBLIC HEARING

There are hearings going on in city councils and state legislatures across America. What may be less publicized are the hearings conducted by different organizations. Some board of astronomers decides whether Pluto is a planet; some charity trustees decide whether to give money to support a homeless shelter; some panel decides whether a building should be a historic landmark. Select a current topic that aligns with your curriculum and ask students to research to find an organization involved with the issue. Have students hold their own hearing on the issue. For example, should college football players be allowed to unionize and be paid for playing? The National Labor Relations Board had a hearing about this. Select some students to be on the NLRB panel, others to present on behalf of the players, and others to present on behalf of the universities. To keep it simple, set up the presentations to focus on one of the thinking skills. Perhaps you want well-constructed arguments or great evidence or demonstrations of rhetorical techniques. Students don't have to prepare for a full-fledged debate but can practice one piece of good thinking.

(Chapter 3, Chapter 5, Chapter 6)

STUDY INFOMERCIALS

If you channel-surf, you know about infomercials. Half-hour or hour-long programs to pitch jewelry, cooking tools, clothing and accessories, exercise equipment, and miracle treatments are vying for your dollars. These are elaborate productions. They may include an attractive host/pitchperson, an expert (doctor, scientist, guru), regular folks offering testimonials, an argument (for example, being overweight is harmful; this product causes weight loss; therefore, buy this product), evidence (graphs, statistics), and persuasive techniques. Place students in teams of four and ask them to create a program. Allow teams to pitch an existing product or to invent a new one. Who plays the host? The expert? What evidence is needed? What persuasive techniques should be used? Students can practice collaboration, media literacy, speaking skills, and thinking skills in this activity.

(Chapter 5, Chapter 6)

PRACTICE DEBATES

As I mentioned in Chapter 1, I have a long history with formal debate. Some years, I set up debate tournaments for my classes. We'd select a topic, do research, choose teams, and follow the strict rules of tournament debate. Student teams would progress through the quarterfinals, semifinals, and finals to crown a champion. Students not participating in the debate on a given day or students whose teams had lost served as judges. The tournament was a long, elaborate process. I thought it was worth the investment of time because students practiced so many valuable skills, including researching, thinking, and speaking. The competition inspired hard work.

Check out the National Association for Urban Debate Leagues. In twenty-two cities across America, middle and high school students have tournament debates as well. My tournament pitted Period Four students against Period Four students. At the Urban Debate League, the competition is much larger. The league selects a topic, and students compete against others at weekend tournaments. These formal competitions are not the only way to debate, however. Let me suggest some simpler ideas.

I wrote about traveling debates in *Well Spoken,* and I update the activity here:

Traveling debates can be used in any subject. The teacher poses a question. Should the character in the novel have done that? Should colleges give in-state tuition to children of undocumented immigrants? Should Uber be regulated? Should cigarettes be banned? Come up with some content-related questions that have two strong sides. Then tell the class to stand up and move: "Stand on this side of the room if you think that we should have physical education every day. Stand on that side of the room if you think we should not have P.E. every day."

It is not important to have an even number of students on each side. In fact, sometimes it is more fun to have five students against twenty-five students. As long as there are people on each side, you can begin. (No, no one can be in the middle—we either have P.E. every day or we don't. Make students decide.)

The rules are simple. One person speaks at a time. I address the side with the smaller number and let someone from that side speak first for one minute or less. The speaker tries to persuade students from the other side to walk over to his side. There is no clapping, no voting, and no commenting—if your viewpoint has changed, you simply move over to the other side of the room. When students finish moving (if they move—sometimes no one is persuaded), call on a student from the opposing side of the room. Her goal is the same: to get students to switch sides. Call on different students from each side several times.

I would usually fit this in at the end of class. Got five or ten minutes to spare? Traveling debate!

Try Pop-Up Debate, an idea invented by Dave Stuart Jr. Present a topic to the class. For instance, should the United States use unmanned drones for military strikes abroad? Use a video to introduce the issue, assign students a side, and send them to ProCon.org (www. procon.org) to research for ten minutes. At the end of ten minutes, start the debate. A student wishing to speak stands up—hence the name Pop-Up Debate—and speaks for one minute. If more than one stands, a moderator points to one person. No one can talk more than once. The talk follows a formula: make a statement, provide a piece of evidence, explain how the evidence supports the statement, and sum up. When the speaker finishes, students with an opposing view can pop up. You can read more about this by searching Dave's website, www.davestuartjr.com/resources/. Other teachers are willing to share their debate activities too. Search online to find other versions.

(Chapter 3, Chapter 4, Chapter 5)

CRITIQUE OTHERS' DEBATES

Many websites focus on debate techniques. I mentioned the Pro/Con site earlier. A similar site is Debate.org (www.debate.org). Students can find engaging topics (for example, should teachers be able to monitor a student's computer?) and read the arguments posted there. They can enter their own opinions. Rather than enter the fray, however, I like the idea of being an impartial observer. *My* opinion is not important right now. I just want to analyze the arguments others have made. Are the arguments well constructed? Is there good evidence to support the position? Let students explore. Ask half of the class to look for great arguments and half to look for flawed arguments. Have volunteers share their discoveries and explain why they chose the examples.

You can also find websites that post videos of debates and have students critique the speakers. At the high end, Intelligence2 Debates (http://intelligencesquaredus.org/) show legal scholars debating current topics. Select snippets that demonstrate the kinds of thinking you want students to emulate. Visit the website of the International Debate Education Association (www.idebate.org). Students from around the world are contributing arguments and voting for the arguments of others about very engaging issues: banning testing on animals, same-sex schools, reality television, assisted suicide, and many more.

(Chapter 3, Chapter 4, Chapter 5)

USE ONLINE TOOLS

I mentioned Intel's Visual Ranking tool in Chapter 6. Intel has a Seeing Reason tool and a Showing Evidence tool (www.intel.com /content/www/us/en/education/k12/teachers.html). These graphic organizers help students visualize some of the thinking processes we have discussed in this book. A web search of "graphic organizer for argument" will locate many samples. They are often flawed, but you can tweak them. For example, if the graphic organizer includes a box labeled "Point to Be Made" leading to three boxes labeled "Reason," each of which leads to three boxes labeled "Example or Fact," you could relabel them, respectively, as "Conclusion," "Statement Leading to the Conclusion," and "Evidence." In the rare case when you get stumped for argumentative prompts, help is available online. Try the *New York Times* learning blog (http://learning.blogs.nytimes.com/2014/02/04/200-prompts-for-argumentative-writing/?_r=0) or similar sites.

Remember the graph in Chapter 7 that compared margarine consumption and divorce? Many similar graphs are found at Spurious Correlations (www.tylervigen.com/spurious-correlations). Let students explore logical fallacies at Thou Shall Not Commit Logical Fallacies (https://yourlogicalfallacyis.com/). Give students the job of looking for similar sites.

(Chapter 3, Chapter 5)

WATCH TV

Television shows provide unusual ways to teach good thinking. Have you seen the show *House Hunters* on HGTV? Viewers watch as real estate agents take prospective home buyers around. I find it odd that audiences willingly watch such a mundane process. Yet the show demonstrates argument in everyday life. Buyers are constantly making arguments:

> *We have kids.*
> *Kids need a good yard.*
> *House A has a good yard.*
> *We want House A.*

But

> *We can't afford more than X.*
> *House A costs more than X.*
> *We can't buy House A.*

So

We have kids.
Kids need a good place to play.
House B is near a park.
We want House B instead.

We can watch buyers think and rethink, and we can use them as examples for teaching. Other reality shows ask, "What is the argument for why I should invest in your company?" and "What is the argument for asking someone to pay a lot of money for that item you found in Grandma's attic?" Let students find other examples.

(Chapter 3)

CONDUCT A PLATONIC SEMINAR

No, that is not a misprint. I know that many people are familiar with Socratic seminars. Most so-called Socratic seminars are simply discussions with a fancy name and bear no resemblance to anything Socrates ever did in ancient Greece. We know about Socrates because Plato wrote a series of "dialogues" in which Socrates was the main character. Those dialogues reveal that Socrates was a very active participant in every discussion, not a teacher sitting back observing. Socrates spoke after every comment! I suggested in *Teaching the Core Skills of Listening & Speaking* (2014) that we should have Platonic seminars using the model Plato observed.

Assign a student or team of students to play the part of Socrates, who has the job of challenging every statement made. If a speaker says, "Drones are an inexpensive way to strike military targets," Socrates will question the speaker.

Do you have numbers showing how much a drone strike costs compared with a traditional strike?
Are there costs besides dollars? Do we lose friends by attacking randomly?
Will innocent people be hurt?

Can drones miss more often than pilots?

Notice that Socrates never states a position. He only questions, but to be sure, the questions may suggest a point of view.
(Chapter 4, Chapter 5)

CONTINUE A DEBATE ONLINE

Some students are silent in class. Perhaps shy, perhaps slower to digest and formulate ideas, or perhaps not confident speakers, these students can be given a digital voice. I love sites that allow discussions to continue online. I was always disturbed that some students seemed shut out of class discussions, and online tools can solve the problem. The two that I share here have a cost, however: a basic Flipgrid account (www.flipgrid.com) is $65.00 as I write this; a VoiceThread account (www.voicethread.com) costs $79.00. If you can come up with the money, these tools are well worth the expense.

At both sites, you create a prompt. Use topics that will engage your students—"Should gum chewing be allowed in class?" "Should cell phones be used for tests?"—or topics that come up during a unit of study. You then give students the web address—the link—to that prompt. At Flipgrid, you can type the prompt, or, much more fun, use your web camera to record a video of yourself explaining the prompt. Students go online, read or watch the prompt, and respond by recording a video. Students can record and rerecord as much as they wish until they get a publishable response. They also can watch the videos of others who completed the assignment before them and respond to those students as well as to the prompt. At some point, there will be a chain of small, personal videos with everyone's opinion showcased.

Set up the prompt to emphasize an individual thinking skill. For one, require a statement and a piece of evidence. For another, require a rhetorical technique. For yet another, require a response to some other student's video comment. For fun, require students to intentionally make a reasoning error—a collection of videos featuring bad generalizations, personal attacks, off-track comments, and more. (I also think you should have an assignment that requires an element of good speaking!)

VoiceThread offers a different approach but a similar result. You create a prompt and give students the link to it. You can type the prompt, record your voice, post a video, and post an image or a link to a website for discussion. Students can respond in those ways as well. The product is not a chain of videos but rather a central page with the prompt and many icons up and down both sides. Clicking on an icon opens a student comment, whether written or recorded.

I have examples of these at www.pvlegs.com.

(Chapter 3, Chapter 5, Chapter 6, Chapter 7)

PRODUCE AN ARGUMENT FOR AN ONLINE AUDIENCE

Check out C-SPAN's StudentCam (www.studentcam.org/). In the words of the site, "StudentCam is C-SPAN's annual national video documentary competition that encourages students to think critically about issues that affect our communities and our nation." Students create five- to seven-minute videos. Show some past winners to your students as an exercise in critiquing argument. The real fun, though, is in creating a video. In an age in which standards demand multimedia presentations and students are increasingly adept at using digital tools, we should look for opportunities such as this. Perhaps your students are not able to compete with the big kids at StudentCam. In that case, make a scaled-down version of the project. Post the videos to your school website or to your classroom site, if you have one.

(Chapter 3, Chapter 5)

LOOK AT THE BIG TEST

We are in the era of high-stakes testing as I write this. Some subsequent edition of this book may omit this activity, but for now, passing the Big Test is a concern for many teachers. My goal in writing this book was quite a bit larger than jumping through the year-end hoop. I want good thinking stressed throughout our students' lives. Still, you should look at some released or practice items that test companies provide. You will be surprised at how minimal the expectations are.

My state is using the Partnership for Assessment of Readiness for College and Careers (PARCC), which has practice tests online. A sixth-grade item asks students to assess arguments about Amelia Earhart's bravery. Students read two articles and watch one video. There are comprehension questions along the way, but ultimately students are asked to compare arguments. It is suggested that all three pieces conclude that Earhart was a brave woman. How well did they build their arguments? Article One: She wasn't scared when a plane swooped by, she wasn't afraid to cross the Atlantic alone, she wasn't afraid to try to go around the world; therefore, she was brave. Article Two: They never found her body, some people think she may have crashed on an atoll; therefore, she was brave. (True, the article has nothing to do with her bravery. I assume it is an intentional decision, making it easy for students to compare: "Article One is a much better argument because the statements support the conclusion. In Article Two, there are no statements to support the conclusion." The only expectation for evidence is to find quotes: "In paragraph one, Earhart stood her ground when a plane swooped at them." By twelfth grade, students build their own arguments. In the practice example, they are asked to state a conclusion about what freedom and independence means and offer statements from readings to support the conclusion.

How do test makers score argument? PARCC's Research Simulation Task rubric wants "clear reasoning supported by relevant text-based evidence." The Smarter Balanced Assessment Consortium, a group that competes with PARCC, essentially uses one writing rubric for all tasks. It is slightly tweaked to make the change from argumentative to informational to opinion writing. "Claim is introduced, clearly communicated" and "comprehensive evidence (facts and details) from the source material is integrated." Or, in our language, "*Conclusion* is introduced, clearly communicated" and "comprehensive *quotes* from the source material are integrated." Expectations are low. "Amelia is brave. She wasn't afraid of the swooping plane (Paragraph One)" should do it. Your students will be able to handle this and much more. Still, it is useful to show them how the test game is played.

(Chapter 3, Chapter 5)

DON'T OVERDO IT

If one of the ideas in this chapter seems more fun or more valuable than something you currently do, try it, but don't feel the need to do everything. I often think that teachers are so buried in new things to try that they become overwhelmed and end up trying nothing. I hope that isn't the result here. Keep these ideas in the back of your mind. Sometime during the year, in the middle of a unit you always teach and always love teaching, an idea will hit you: *Hey, I could add a thinking lesson here and try out that activity I read about in Erik's book!* My goal is to empower students with good thinking skills, not to overwhelm teachers.

Afterword

I ended the book *Well Spoken* by referencing an old comedy routine. In the routine, Father Guido Sarducci speaks about starting the Five-Minute University. His claim is that in five minutes, you can learn everything that the average college graduate remembers five years after leaving school. That routine haunted me all through my teaching career. Do you mean that all my hard work, all my brilliant lesson plans, and all my fifty-five-hour weeks were for nothing? They're going to forget almost everything I taught them? I strived every day to teach something that I thought would last. I knew that students would forget some of what I taught them. But I also wanted them to be able to say in the future, "You know, Mr. Palmer taught me some things I've never forgotten."

We would still know all the lessons we have forgotten if they mattered to us. I have forgotten about the layers of the atmosphere, but a meteorologist remembers them. I don't recall the quadratic formula, but a math teacher does. What can we guarantee will matter to the lives of *all* our students? I know that every day they will value learning to speak well. I know they will be grateful that we taught them to think well, too.

Employers will not ask our students to write haikus or name the metalloids in the periodic table. Success in society will not depend upon our ability to recite the dates of the Punic Wars or a sonnet from Shakespeare. This is not to say that those things should not be part of education. The fallible memory of adults does not mean there is no value in what we were taught. Yet if we want to spend a minute pondering what skills will be valued by employers and by society, I am confident that the ability to think well will be on the list.

Consider the ideas shared in this book. Are there any that wouldn't benefit all of your students? Building arguments, analyzing arguments, supporting statements with evidence, being aware of persuasive and rhetorical tricks, looking for errors of reasoning? Which of these seems superfluous? All occur in adult lives. Evaluate the proposal. Figure out whom to vote for. Persuade your sixteen-year-old to drive carefully. Tell a student's parents why they need to be more involved in the child's education. Make sense of the barrage of messages that assaults you daily. Analyze whether what I am saying in this afterword makes sense. It might be difficult to come up with examples of when we *aren't* called upon to think.

You are in a position to improve lives. Perhaps you are also in a position to improve the world—a grand thought, indeed. Our era is strong on persuasive and rhetorical tricks but weak on logic and reasoning. We have neglected to teach those skills, and it shows. The caliber of argument used by the founders of our country is much higher than the caliber of national discourse today. How did such brilliant thinking devolve into what we read and hear nowadays? You can begin the process of putting us back on track. Teach children the keys to good thinking.

REFERENCES

American Association of Neurological Surgeons. www.aans.org
/patient%20information/conditions%20and%20treatments
/concussion.aspx.

Common Core State Standards Initiative. 2010. *Common Core State
Standards for English Language Arts & Literacy in History/Social
Studies, Science, and Technical Subjects:* Washington, DC: CCSSO &
National Governors Association. www.corestandards.org/other
-resources/key-shifts-in-english-language-arts/.

Crider, Scott F. 2005. *The Office of Assertion: An Art of Rhetoric for the
Academic Essay.* Wilmington, DE: ISI Books.

Doyle, Arthur Conan. 2012. Sherlock Holmes series. B&R Samizdat
Express.

Fletcher, James. 2014. "Spurious Correlations: Margarine Linked to
Divorce?" BBC News, May 26. www.bbc.com/news
/magazine-27537142.

Himmelman, Jeff. 2013. "A Game of Shark and Minnow." *New York Times
Magazine*, October 27. www.nytimes.com/newsgraphics/2013/10/27
/south-china-sea/.

Indiana Academic Standards. 2014. www.doe.in.gov/sites/default/files
/standards/mathematics/2014-07-31-math-g7-architecturewith
-front-matter_br.pdf.

Intel. Visual Ranking Tool. www.intel.com/content/www/us/en
/education/k12/thinking-tools/visual-ranking.html.

Murphy, Ryan. *Men's Fitness.* www.mensfitness.com/life/sports/10
-most-superstitious-athletes.

Palmer, Erik. 2011. *Well Spoken: Teaching Speaking to All Students.* Portland, ME: Stenhouse.

——. 2014. *Teaching the Core Skills of Listening & Speaking.* Alexandria, VA: ASCD.

Progressive Insurance. 2002. "Claims Survey Finds There's No Place Like Home-for Vehicle Crashes." www.progressive.com/newsroom /article/2002/may/fivemiles/.

Salmon, Wesley C. 1963. *Logic.* Englewood Cliffs, NJ: Prentice-Hall.

Sharecare, Inc. "How Dangerous Is Secondhand Smoke?" www .sharecare.com/health/quit-smoking/how-dangerous-second-hand -smoke.

Steele, Brian. 2015. "Supreme Court Same-Sex Marriage Ruling: WNEU Law Professor Agrees with Legal Reasoning." www.masslive.com /news/index.ssf/2015/06/wneu_law_professor_agrees_with.html.

Texas Essential Knowledge and Skills. Texas Education Agency. Chapter 110. Texas Essential Knowledge and Skills for English Language Arts and Reading Subchapter A. Elementary. http://ritter .tea.state.tx.us/rules/tac/chapter110/ch110a.html#110.12.

Wilson, Iain. 2014. "Bloomberg Business China's Solar Power Push." www.bloomberg.com/bw/articles/2014-11-06/chinas-solar-power -push.